The Obvious Candidate

Land Your Dream Job, Get Paid More To Do It, and Take Command Of Your Career!

Tommy West

COPYRIGHT

The Obvious Candidate, by Tommy West, copyright © 2024 by Job Seekers University, LLC.

All rights reserved.

No part of this book may be reproduced, distributed, uploaded, or used for training AI without permission of the author, except as permitted by copyright law.

Tommy West reserves the right to be identified as the author of this work.

Published by: Game Changer Publishing.

Paperback ISBN: 978-1-964811-62-8
Hardcover ISBN: 978-1-964811-63-5
Digital ISBN: 978-1-964811-64-2

CONTENTS

DEDICATION 1

INTRODUCTION: ARE YOU READY TO LAND YOUR DREAM JOB? 3

CHAPTER 1: DEBUNKING THE 5 MYTHS OF THE OLD WAY OF JOB SEARCHING 25

CHAPTER 2: THE DREAM JOB FORMULA 45

CHAPTER 3: GET THE UNFAIR ADVANTAGE 77

CHAPTER 4: BECOME INSTANTLY NOTICED 105

CHAPTER 5: GET PAST THE GATEKEEPERS 129

CHAPTER 6: THE ONE: HOW TO STAND OUT AGAINST YOUR COMPETITION AND WIN THE FINAL STAGES OF YOUR JOB SEARCH 153

CHAPTER 7: HOW TO ADD THOUSANDS TO YOUR FINAL SALARY 187

CHAPTER 8: A SPECIAL SURPRISE FOR YOU! 207

THANK YOU! 225

JOIN OUR CAREER COMMANDERS TRIBE! 227

CONTACT OUR EXPERTS 229

ACKNOWLEDGMENTS 231

ABOUT THE AUTHOR 233

MORE GREAT CONTENT BY TOMMY WEST 235

DEDICATION

I dedicate this book to every job seeker who believes they can land their dream job and take command of their career. (You can!)

I also dedicate this book to my grandmother, Judith Davies—a true pioneer in the advancement of Career Transition services and trailblazer in women's Executive Leadership.

INTRODUCTION: ARE YOU READY TO LAND YOUR DREAM JOB?

Welcome to my book, *The Obvious Candidate: Land Your Dream Job, Get Paid More To Do It, and Take Command Of Your Career!*

I'm Tommy West, and I'm honored and excited that you've decided to invest in your career by starting this book!

As my book title indicates, I wrote this book to help you transform yourself into what I call the OBVIOUS CANDIDATE! In doing that—again, as my title assures you—I'll help you fast track landing the job of your dreams, earn more money, and take command of your career.

But how? I've created a 5-step process that we'll explore in these pages to help you become the Obvious Candidate, all without suffering through countless applications and demoralizing rejection.

In fact, I'm on a mission to free 1 million job seekers from the chains of traditional job search methods and help them permanently take back command over their careers. Why? Because I believe that you DESERVE better.

It takes U.S. job seekers an average of 5 months to land a job, most of which AREN'T their dream jobs. Also, 82% of Americans say searching for a new job is an extremely stressful experience.

Something needs to change, and until now, there wasn't a way out. But over the first 5 chapters of this book, I'm going to show you there IS a way out. And better yet, you'll see just how quick and effortless it can be to land the job of your dreams, get paid more to do it, and put the power back into your hands.

MY 5-STEP FRAMEWORK TO BECOME THE OBVIOUS CANDIDATE

In this book, I want to give you my proven job search system that's helped thousands go from frustrated job seekers to CAREER COMMANDERS. In the first 5 chapters, you're going to learn and implement my 5-step framework to immediately make you the Obvious Candidate, and ultimately, land your dream job. (Each of the 5 steps corresponds to the first 5 chapters). I've also packed two awesome bonus chapters into the back of this book to give you an UNFAIR ADVANTAGE in the final stages of your job search, but for now, let's only focus on just the first 5 chapters.

I believe that the information I've packed into my system I'm about to share is REVOLUTIONARY. It has NEVER been shared before in this format because it's typically only available to those going through company-sponsored programs or wealthy corporate executives.

Here's a rundown of what we'll explore in the first 5 chapters of this book.

In **Step 1 / Chapter 1**, I'll show you all about the MYTHS we've been sold about how to search for jobs. I'll also uncover exactly WHY the job search process makes you feel like you're stuck in the middle of an endless cycle, a process that leaves you with more questions than answers.

In **Step 2 / Chapter 2**, I'll show you how to sidestep the pitfalls that cause mainstream job searches to fail. I'll also reveal how to beat their broken systems by using my DREAM JOB FORMULA. It took me years of constant researching, refining, and trial and error to create this formula, and I can't wait to reveal it to you.

In **Step 3 / Chapter 3**, I'll show you how to create an UNFAIR ADVANTAGE for yourself against other job applicants. Now to be clear, when I say unfair, I don't mean biased or dishonest. I simply mean that you'll have an unfair advantage over others by learning that you actually don't need to be the most qualified or experienced candidate to land your dream job. You just need to be the most OBVIOUS candidate.

In **Step 4 / Chapter 4**, I'll show you how to become INSTANTLY NOTICED by your top companies and reveal the 2 visibility hacks that will have recruiters and hiring managers attracted to you like a magnet.

In **Step 5 / Chapter 5**, I'll pull back the curtain and ensure your application gets PAST the GATEKEEPERS (HR managers, applicant tracking systems, hiring boards, etc.).

YOUR OUTCOMES

What outcomes can you expect from my 5-step framework to make you the Obvious Candidate in this book?

I've already mentioned that I wrote this book to help you land your DREAM JOB, earn MORE MONEY, and take COMMAND of your CAREER, all without suffering through countless applications and facing constant rejection. But what does that really mean? What tangible results will you actually get from this book?

Clarity is paramount in landing your dream job. In the following paragraphs, I've bolded each instance of the word clarity to highlight the exact outcomes you'll get from each of the first 5 chapters in this book.

In **Step 1 / Chapter 1**, you'll get clarity on how to fix the broken job search process and immediately put the power back into your hands.

In **Step 2 / Chapter 2**, you'll get clarity on how my DREAM JOB FORMULA unifies your job search. In doing so, you'll get clarity on how to become the OBVIOUS Candidate to your key decision-makers, whether they are recruiters, hiring managers, the board of directors, or someone else.

In **Step 3 / Chapter 3**, you'll get clarity on how to market and sell yourself so that you go from being a run-of-the-mill candidate to the MOST OBVIOUS Candidate. You'll also get clarity on why it's ok that there'll always be someone better than you. Instead of wasting time trying to fight against how things are, you'll get clarity on WHY your qualifications and experiences that are listed in your resume or LinkedIn Profile often aren't what gets you the job.

In **Step 4 / Chapter 4**, you'll get clarity on how to drop the dull candidate persona, and become a MAGNETIC CANDIDATE. Your days of chasing recruiters and hiring managers will be over. After you apply the lessons from this chapter, it'll be like a switch has flipped on in your job search process. In fact, you may even have to turn your search process OFF because you'll have too much interest and too many interview requests.

In **Step 5 / Chapter 5**, you'll get clarity on how to get PAST the GATEKEEPERS and drastically increase your chances of making it into your dream job's final round of candidates.

WHAT DOES SUCCESS LOOK LIKE FOR YOU?

If you want to land your dream job, commitment is key. I want you to commit to doing whatever it takes to land it. I want you to commit to yourself, your family, and friends (and maybe your colleagues, too!) that you are a CAREER COMMANDER who deserves a fulfilling, well-paid job.

But, honestly, for this to work, I can't just TELL you to be committed. You have to DECIDE to commit and then FULLY BELIEVE that you are indeed committed.

So, before we go on, I urge you to check in with yourself to assess if you are or aren't committed. Do so by asking yourself the following questions:

- Do I really want to land my dream job?

- Do I really want to get paid for what I'm worth?

- Do I really want to take command of my career?

As you'll surely notice, the previous questions correspond exactly to the subtitle of this book, which is, *Land Your Dream Job, Get Paid More To Do It, and Take Command Of Your Career!*

To really gauge your commitment levels, here are some additional questions I encourage you to answer:

- Will I do everything it takes to bypass the normal, grueling 6-month-long process to find a job?

- Will I never settle for an average, unfulfilling job again?

- Will I commit to getting the exciting and rewarding job that I know I deserve?

So, are you in or are you out?

If you're out, I wish you the best of luck in your job search journey. Also, I want you to know you're always welcome back into our Career Commander community if you want a better, easier way.

If you're in and you're committed, great! Congratulations! It's time to put the power back into your hands and take command over your career.

Additionally, on both a personal and professional note, THANK YOU for trusting me to be your guide. I don't take this responsibility lightly.

COMMIT TO DOING ALL OF THE 5-STEPS IN THIS BOOK

There's a WRONG way to read this book. The wrong way would be letting distractions get in the way of your success (put down your phone!), procrastinating (stop streaming movies!), and thinking that you'll just pick up this book tomorrow (will you, really?).

I wrote each of the first 5 chapters in this book to give you a precise path to finding your dream job. At the end of each chapter, I've created some challenging exercises to ensure you practically explore the content of the chapters. I call these end-of-chapter exercises CAREER COMMANDER ASSIGNMENTS. They're very important. Don't skip them. Make sure you do them!

The RIGHT way to approach this book is to play to WIN and give it 100%. Read every chapter and then complete each exercise in the end-of-chapter CAREER COMMANDER ASSIGNMENTS.

WHAT MAKES MY 5-STEP FRAMEWORK DIFFERENT?

I've made some bold claims that my 5-step framework will help you become the Obvious Candidate, and ultimately land your dream job. So what makes my process different from everything else you've ever heard?

Out there in what I playfully yet scornfully call the PROFESSIONAL RECRUITMENT INDUSTRIAL COMPLEX, there are tons of people who want to give you advice and take your money. They've got countless strategies and "tested" methods about how to find your dream job.

But they rarely solve all of your job search needs. Nearly without exception, they just give you one piece of a much larger puzzle. They fail at providing a COMPREHENSIVE framework and system that solves the various problems you'll face in landing your dream job.

Another major problem of the Professional Recruitment Industrial Complex is that it primarily benefits the CONSULTANTS that job seekers pay and the COMPANIES that end up hiring them. Sound familiar? That stops here. The system should benefit the JOB SEEKER.

The traditional (i.e. The Old Way) of job searching puts YOU in a terrible spot by making you think you're the problem.

But you're NOT. The entire job search process, from its very beginning, has been setting you up for failure, not success. It's the existing system that doesn't work.

I feel compassion for the so-called experts who teach the traditional, old way of job searching. They don't know anything else. They're simply relaying what they've been taught. They want to focus on just one part of the job search process and provide you with "suggestions." They don't want to admit that looking at the entire process reveals that it consists of various linked steps, all interdependent on each other for success.

Also, companies and their HR departments use processes and technology that work AGAINST you to make THEIR lives easier. What they SHOULD be doing is trying to find the best candidate. But they prefer to use software—called Applicant Tracking Systems—to filter out job applicants to make their hiring decisions easier.

So, if you're wondering why you're not making it to the interview stage for your dream job, or why you have to start all over after each rejected application, it's because you're a victim of a BROKEN system.

Over these next 5 chapters, I'm going to show you that you absolutely CAN land YOUR DREAM JOB, the job you truly desire and deserve, and the process doesn't need to take an average of 5 months and be full of rejection, tiresome work, and endless waiting.

You just need the RIGHT system. My 5-step framework to becoming the Obvious Candidate and landing your dream job IS the core of that system. And it's exactly what I'm going to show you throughout the first 5 chapters of this book. (Reminder: I've also got some bonus chapters at the back of the book. But as I mentioned, let's tackle one thing at a time and put our focus on these first chapters to make you the Obvious Candidate.)

WHO NEEDS A JOB SEARCH SYSTEM?

I've talked to numerous job seekers who think they should just play the (old) game that the recruiters want them to play. Here are various statements that "doomed-before-they-start" job seekers have said to me:

- "I don't need a job search system."

- "Shouldn't I just submit my resume to around one hundred jobs and hope I get an interview or two?"

- "Shouldn't I just improve my skills to make myself more attractive to employers?"

- "Shouldn't I just network and make more industry connections?"

In my experience, EVERYONE needs a system that will unify each part of their search process, thus making them the MOST OBVIOUS CANDIDATE in the eyes of their dream companies.

The right system is needed by:

- Recent graduates.

- Mid-level professionals.

- Executives.

- People who want a career change.

- People who are returning to the workforce, including those who have been laid-off.

- Freelancers.

Really, the right system is needed by ANYONE who wants to put the power back into their hands and take command over their careers.

WHAT IS A SUCCESSFUL JOB SEARCH?

If you're looking for a job, the best OUTCOME of that process is landing a job. In other words, getting the job is the most successful RESULT. But what about the PROCESS itself?

Do you know what a successful job search process should look like?

I've asked this question to countless people. Their various responses tell me that there is a lot of GUESSWORK around WHAT a successful job search looks like. I've received answers to this question like:

- "It's all about your resume."

- "You have to know the right people."

- "You have to figure out how to get your resume past those pesky filters companies use."

If your answer included something like one of the previous answers, you're on the right track. The tricky thing is that a successful job search process incorporates ALL of the above steps, and MORE, albeit differently than you may think.

The goal is to use each of the above parts within your own job search process. But we can't just rehash the old ways.

In the world of job searching, there have always been videos that give you advice, coaches that guide you, and resources that assist with things like improving your resume. As I've mentioned, I bundle this all together and call it The OLD Way of Job Searching.

But what if they are EXACTLY what's holding you back? More importantly, what if there was a way to change how you search for jobs—getting rid of The Old Way and its stressful, timely, and broken results forever?

The 5-step framework and system I'm giving you in this book isn't just advice. It's a tailored roadmap full of action every step of the way—ensuring that you're not just walking, but sprinting to the job of your dreams.

My new system effectively does the heavy lifting for you. It eliminates the guesswork and positions you directly in front of employers and roles that align with your passions and skills.

My new system provides you with access to exclusive tools that were previously only available to people who participate in exclusive, corporate-sponsored programs. These tools will level the playing field and directly put the power back into your hands.

THIS is The New Way. As ONE unified system, it replaces the Old Way for GOOD.

WHO AM I? AND WHY SHOULD YOU LISTEN TO ME?

The system I'll be uncovering in the first 5 chapters of this book is the direct result of helping thousands of job seekers find their Unfair Advantage, become the Obvious Candidate, and ultimately land their dream jobs in record time.

But before we jump into my system, I'd like to tell you a little about myself so that you can decide for yourself to trust me and know for sure that I'm qualified enough to guide you through this process. Trust is a huge factor for me, and I know it is for you as well. And it's important to know that the people, like me, you're learning from have the results to back it up!

But that wasn't always me. In fact, just a few short years ago, I was struggling through my own job search—wondering why I felt invisible and trapped in a process that seemed like it would never end.

You see, I've actually been exposed to the struggles job seekers face my entire life. Growing up, my family's business was to provide career transition services for the employees of companies who were conducting layoffs. But it was never something I thought I would be so passionate about myself.

Until I graduated from college, my focus was on being a student athlete who played baseball and trying to figure out what life held for me after that. And because NCAA regulations wouldn't allow me to get a full-time job until I graduated, my summers consisted of working part-time in the family business.

To be completely honest with you, I didn't enjoy it. I liked working with job seekers. But the overall process was slow and didn't seem to have much impact. It was a problem that was easy to pass off on other people, and one at the time I really didn't give much thought to since I was about to graduate, end my baseball career, and was just searching to find a path that gave me a sense of fulfillment.

I wanted a job that I loved, paid well, and gave me purpose. Isn't that what we all want?

Here's the thing. When I graduated from college, I thought that I knew all the secrets and that getting a job would be a breeze.

Boy was I wrong. In fact, I was blindsided. Despite my background and determination, I spiraled into what I now call the JOB SEARCH CRAZY CYCLE. Months went by, rejection emails flooded in, and unanswered applications left a deafening silence that made me feel invisible.

After months of feeling like a failure, I got lucky—a family friend referred me to their company, which hired me. Saved! I never wanted to go through the terrible, painful process of searching for a job ever again.

Once I got that job, I was completely fulfilled and earned tons of money. HA! NOPE. The job was very far from my dream job, and I hated the prospect of jumping back into a search process that had cost me so much time, stress, and anxiety.

It was in this situation, though, where everything changed. The day was Friday, June 16th, 2017, and almost all of the management team was out of the office that day for a big corporate event. Of course, this meant an unfiltered free-for-all opportunity to discuss anything and everything in the office was about to take place, right?!

For my introverted nature, this was a nightmare. But for my VERY extroverted co-worker sitting in the cubicle behind me, this could've been Thanksgiving Day Part 2. In fact, I got a front row seat to several conversations that would change the course and purpose of my life forever.

Still feeling stuck between the reality of being unfulfilled in my job and the fear of not wanting to go through the job search process again, I was in for a surprise. I was not alone. Almost all of my colleagues felt the same way as me. I overheard numerous conversations of people venting about their jobs, things like:

- "They're not treating me right here."

- "I don't like working here."

- "I'm nowhere near paid enough for the time and effort I put into this job."

My colleague would ask the people complaining why they didn't find a new job somewhere else. They'd give their reasons, such as:

- "What, and go through that torture of finding a job again?"
- "But I have security here."
- "I don't have the time to change jobs."

Quickly I realized that their excuses were EXACTLY THE SAME as my excuses.

Everyone—including myself—would rather stay in a job they hated to avoid experiencing all the pain of searching for a new job.

It dawned on me that I wasn't the only one who couldn't stand searching for jobs. And that's when I finally felt my CALLING. I wanted to make sure that no other job seeker ever had to feel the same way that I—and so many others—did again.

So, I did the one thing I never thought I'd do—I quit my job and went back to my family company. But this time was very different from before. Now, not only did I understand the pains of the job search from a first-hand perspective, but I had also directly seen how many people it held back from the careers they truly desired and deserved—before they even started looking for a job!

So I immediately got to work and asked myself a question that would ultimately spark me to create the system I'm sharing with you in this book: How can this process be better?

Over the next few years, I invested thousands of hours helping hundreds of different job seekers. Every day, I immersed myself in their job search processes. With each person, I relentlessly tested my strategies, frameworks, and methods.

Finding problems was easy. However, figuring out HOW to fix them was extremely hard. I started to understand WHY no one had dared challenge The Old Way of job searching. Because to fix it, the ENTIRE process needed to be changed.

It needed to have the right foundation. It needed to be unified. And it needed to work FOR job seekers, not AGAINST them.

So, I flipped every part upside down. I pushed aside everything I was taught about how the job search process "should" work.

Often I failed. Hard. When helping job seekers who didn't get their dream jobs, I wanted to give up. Their rejection felt like my rejection. Gradually though, over the years, I could see the whole process with clarity. And a new system started to emerge that I tested and refined on thousands of job seekers—from entry-level positions to executives at Fortune 500 companies.

The long-term results of this system have far exceeded even my wildest expectations. When creating this system, it was my mission to solve the broken search process so you could bypass all the stress and heartache associated with it.

But what I've really found—and am most proud of—is that my system, The New Way, has given thousands the key to having complete and total command over their careers. It doesn't just radically change your job search. It unlocks your ability to really understand what makes YOU unique, and in turn, know how to MARKET and SELL yourself. The two most important things you can learn to permanently change the trajectory of your career.

This is what it's all about. It's more than just a 5 step framework and system. It's a movement and The New Way. It's one that transformed me from a frustrated worker who felt invisible to a fulfilled guide who helps others successfully navigate their job search journey. It's one that started with the intent to break the chains of the traditional ways of job searching and provide a better way.

And it's now the cornerstone of my mission to free 1 million job seekers from their current situation and create a community of what I call, "Career Commanders."

I truly believe that EVERYONE can obtain the job they truly desire and deserve.

My fool-proof system can be followed by ANYONE. Whether you're just starting out in your career, going through a huge career change, or are a seasoned executive, it WILL work for you.

Whether you want to Do-it-Yourself—which we'll be covering in this book—or have my team of Job Search Architects and I do your job search FOR you, it WILL work for you.

It's a step-by-step system that takes job seekers from untrusting and hesitant to confident and ready to land their dream job.

I can't wait for you to put these secrets to play in your own life so you can land the job of your dreams!

BEFORE WE JUMP INTO STEP 1 OF MY 5-STEP FRAMEWORK ...

Before we get into the gold that I promised you, I'd like to ask you a question. Where do you really want to be after reading this book?

Put another way, do you want to be in the SAME place you are right now? Or would you love to be looking back with CLARITY because you know the exact dream job you want, and you have a clear path of landing it in DAYS, not months?

In 2023, Rachel got unexpectedly laid-off from a company where she saw herself staying forever. She needed a new job FAST. She applied for tons of jobs. Sometimes she received rejections. Sometimes the (completely unprofessional) companies didn't even let her know that she didn't get the job.

She received no invites to a job interview. Clearly she wasn't getting the result she wanted. That's when she decided she needed to try a different approach.

She reached out to me, and she went through the same system you're going to learn in this book. In no time, she landed her dream job—all while planning her wedding!

This is why I do what I do. I help people like Rachel—and you—land the job of their dreams and not be stressed out about where their next paycheck is coming from.

Are you ready, like Rachel, to commit to finishing the steps in this book to land your DREAM JOB? I recommend you commit RIGHT NOW to finishing this book. And remember, by "finishing" I mean both reading the chapters and completing the exercises (which I call Career Commander Assignments) at the end of each chapter.

If you are ready, I promise that by the end of this book you're going to know exactly how to land your dream job without suffering through countless applications or facing constant rejection-or even needing to be an expert resume writer, interviewer, or networker.

Sound good? Let's make you the Obvious Candidate.

CHAPTER 1: DEBUNKING THE 5 MYTHS OF THE OLD WAY OF JOB SEARCHING

In the Introduction, I gave a high-level overview of the differences between the OUTDATED, Old Way of Job Searching, and The New Way of Job Searching. In this chapter, I'm going to dive into a more detailed view. Remember, I'm not here to highlight your pain and leave you hanging on an actual solution. I'm here to give you the system and framework you need to immediately implement what you're learning into your job search to get RESULTS.

Specifically, in this chapter, we'll explore and debunk the 5 MYTHS of The Old Way of Job Searching. These false beliefs are causing your search process to spin like a broken record and work AGAINST you.

Then we'll uncover the 5 TRUTHS of The New Way of Job Searching. These are the insider secrets that work FOR you and will change how you view and approach your job search—and career—forever.

MYTH 1: IT WILL TAKE YOU MONTHS TO FIND A JOB

The first MYTH that's holding your job search back is something I call the **Never-Ending Quest**.

Here is the MYTH: *A successful job search is a lengthy marathon, averaging around 5 months of work. It's a natural part of the process and should be expected.*

Millions of job seekers fall victim to this limiting belief, which sets them back months of valuable time.

(By the way, do you know who surveyed thousands of American job seekers to figure out that, on average, it takes around 5 months for someone to find a job? The survey was conducted by Randstad USA, which is part of a multi-billion dollar international recruiting company that SPECIALIZES in job searching The OLD WAY! To find the survey where I sourced this statistic, just Google: "Job Hunting Is At Least A 5-Month Slog.")

TRUTH 1: YOU CAN LAND YOUR DREAM JOB IN DAYS, NOT MONTHS

Here is the TRUTH: *Landing your dream job quickly is not just a possibility, but a tangible reality if you take the right APPROACH, have the right TOOLS, and use the right SYSTEM.*

Yes, the data suggests that, all through the country, the average job search process takes around 5 months. But that drawn-out timeline is a byproduct of outdated, fragmented methods based on SUBPAR guidance that gets SUBPAR results. That data does not accurately reflect job seekers who use a GREAT system and get GREAT results.

When you follow my framework that unifies each part of your job search and views it as a whole—rather than separate challenges—and gives you the actionable guidance and resources that do the hard work FOR you, landing your dream job is a much QUICKER and LESS STRESSFUL process than The Old Way likes to portray.

MYTH 2: YOU CAN MASS-APPLY WITH ONE EXCELLENT RESUME

The second MYTH is what I call the **One-and-Done Resume**.

Here is the MYTH: *You just need one, really solid resume to cover all your bases. And once you create it, you can use it to apply for as many jobs as possible.*

Unfortunately, the reality is that this "mass production" mindset drastically HURTS the effectiveness of your application process.

The average American company receives over 250 resumes for EVERY SINGLE JOB OPENING. Their dirty little secret is that the small handful of them that they read aren't picked by HUMANS, they're picked by a MACHINE—the Applicant Tracking System, or ATS for short.

And the primary thing the ATS cares about is how well the EXACT keywords in your resume match the EXACT keywords in their job description. Synonyms don't count. You could be the best applicant for a job, but if you don't hit their keyword match rate, your resume will be rejected by the ATS and never seen by a human.

TRUTH 2: YOU NEED A CUSTOMIZED RESUME FOR MOST OF YOUR APPLICATIONS

Here is the TRUTH: *While you don't need to create a brand-new resume from scratch for each job application, it is imperative to create a base resume that you then quickly customize for each application to ensure it passes the Applicant Tracking System (ATS).*

In my system, I'll teach you how to build a base resume that you can easily personalize so that it passes the Applicant Tracking System (ATS). Plus I'll show you how to write your resume to ensure it HOOKS the key decision-makers at your top opportunities and lands you an interview.

It's going to be the difference-maker that single-handedly saves you MONTHS in your job search process.

Remember, while you may be competing against 249 other resumes for each one of your dream jobs—your competition isn't as tough as you think. Using my framework, you'll be part of the very small percentage of applicants—usually around 2%—who have a tailored resume that both passes the ATS screening and scores you a job interview.

MYTH 3: YOU NEED TO MEET EVERY JOB QUALIFICATION TO APPLY

The third MYTH is what I call the **Perfect Fit Fallacy**.

Here's the MYTH: *You need to meet every single qualification listed in a job posting to apply.*

This damaging belief holds back countless job seekers—because they decide not to apply for a dream job because they've been tricked into believing that since they don't have experience in all the "required" areas, their application will be rejected.

I explore and debunk this myth extensively in chapter 3, but I want to let you know this very important reason why this myth is a falsehood: People DON'T HIRE based on LOGIC. They HIRE based on EMOTION.

TRUTH 3: YOU DON'T NEED TO BE THE MOST QUALIFIED CANDIDATE TO LAND YOUR DREAM JOB

Here is the TRUTH: *You DON'T have to be the most qualified or experienced candidate—you just have to be the MOST OBVIOUS candidate.*

You might be the absolute best at what you do, which would make you hands down the best candidate for a job. However, you're probably more like the rest of us. And for the rest of us, there's always going to be someone more qualified or experienced than us—but that doesn't mean that person will land the job.

In fact, for various reasons, companies often DON'T hire the most QUALIFIED candidate. You may have even experienced this when someone with less experience or skills got the job over you. It's quite possible they were hired because the recruiter or hiring manager figured—rightly or wrongly—that you were OVER qualified for the job, and thus might get bored with it.

More importantly, that person got the job because they knew how to position, market, and sell themselves as the MOST OBVIOUS choice over all the other candidates.

MYTH 4: TO NETWORK, YOU NEED TO BE EXTROVERTED AND WELL-CONNECTED

The fourth MYTH is what I call the **Networking Illusion**.

Here's the MYTH: *To be an effective networker, you need to be extroverted and well-connected. Therefore, if you're introverted or not well-connected, you'll struggle to make meaningful connections and advance your career.*

You might believe that networking seems like an exclusive "Boy's Club" with rules and norms that only insiders know about. Well, you've been sold a lie.

TRUTH 4: YOU CAN BECOME A MASTER NETWORKER FROM BEHIND YOUR OWN COMPUTER SCREEN

Here is the TRUTH: *Networking can sometimes be difficult, but there is a way to approach it where you can minimize all the awkwardness and stress that comes with reaching out to people and making connections with them.*

Networking is the fastest and most direct way to land your dream job. In the industry, when someone you know refers you to the key decision-makers at your target company, you become known as a REFERRED CANDIDATE. Generally, referred candidates make up 7% of all job applicants, yet account for a WHOPPING 40% of ALL HIRES.

You can become a master networker and connect with influential people who then refer you positively to your target companies. And you can do this just about entirely from behind your computer. Yes, you can attend in-person networking events, but you can also use online platforms and social media to expand your network exponentially.

So, how do you go from a random outsider to an INSTANT INSIDER? It all centers around finding your IDEAL REFERRAL—that being the person who will vouch for you to the key decision-makers at your target companies.

To connect with your ideal referral, you don't need to become an expert at cold calling or emailing strangers.

It requires two things: Finding People who both WANT to help you and CAN help you—and then Finding and Creating Commonality with them.

Now, who are those people, and how can you find them? Well, starting with those who WANT to help you—these are your Personal and Peer Connections that you've made throughout your life. Close friends, colleagues, alumni, and others with whom you have a shared affiliation.

But only a few of them will turn into your Ideal Referral because they also need to meet the second piece of criteria—being someone who CAN help you—which means that they work at your target company.

And while you may think your network isn't big enough, or that you won't know anyone to ask at your target company, think again. Because in my system, I'm going to show you exactly WHERE to find them—and better yet, you'll learn how to Find and Create Commonality with ANYONE without ever having to speak to them in person—regardless if you know them or not.

And as a result, you will never struggle to find Ideal Referrals who can instantly position you as the TOP candidate for your dream job ever again!

Does that sound good, or what?!

MYTH 5: JOB INTERVIEWS ARE COMPLETELY OUT OF YOUR CONTROL

The fifth MYTH is what I call the **Out-of-Control Interview**.

Here's the MYTH: *Job interviews are a game of chance, so the best way to prepare for them is to practice non-stop to try to control all potential outcomes, including memorizing tons of answers to various potential questions.*

When job seekers buy into this lie, they sabotage their chances of having a successful interview before it ever begins. They do this by preparing for their interviews with the unrealistic goal of trying to control things that they CAN'T actually control—such as preparing for every question they might be asked and then memorizing and rehearsing each answer.

TRUTH 5: CONTROL IS FOUND WHEN YOU KNOW HOW TO ANSWER ANY QUESTIONS YOU'RE ASKED

Here is the TRUTH: *When preparing for interviews, you should focus less on what the interviewer might ask you and more on what you need to say to get your desired result from the interviewer.*

If you want to gain an unfair advantage in your job interviews, you have to realize that you LOSE control when you prepare for what questions you MIGHT be asked. And you GAIN control when you understand the process of HOW to answer any question you're asked.

You should be crafting your response around the desired outcome you want the INTERVIEWER to take—not what YOU want to say.

For example, if the interviewer says to you, "Tell me about yourself," you should have a proven answering path that shows them you're the OBVIOUS CANDIDATE. To achieve this, during interview preparation, ask yourself:

- "What do I want the interviewer to DO as a result of my answer?"
- "What does the interviewer need to BELIEVE to take that action?"
- "What evidence do I need to use to PROVE it to be true?"

A first-of-its-kind answering framework that I'm SUPER excited to share with you later on in this book!

BONUS MYTH 6: THE SALARY YOU'RE OFFERED IS NON-NEGOTIABLE

Now that I've exposed the 5 MYTHS of The OLD Way of Job Searching and shown how you can overcome them with the 5 TRUTHS of The NEW Way of Job Searching, there's one more special bonus myth and truth that I've saved for the very end.

Conquering this myth will help you add thousands of dollars to your final salary.

The sixth MYTH is what I call the **Salary Trap**.

Here's the MYTH: *Once you're offered a job, you should take the salary offered and definitely not ask for more.*

Pretty much everything in life is negotiable. But for some reason, countless job applicants have been tricked into believing that the salary they're offered is NON-NEGOTIABLE. Furthermore, they often believe that attempting to negotiate a better salary risks LOSING the job to another candidate.

TRUTH 6: YOU CAN (AND SHOULD!) NEGOTIATE YOUR SALARY BEFORE ACCEPTING A JOB OFFER

Here is the TRUTH: *Companies actually ANTICIPATE that applicants will insist on negotiating their salary. That's why companies leave themselves financial wiggle room in the initial offer. But, whenever an applicant takes the offer as-is without asking for more, all of that potential salary NEVER makes it into the applicant's bank account.*

Remember, to the company, your salary is not personal. No one involved in the hiring process—from the hiring manager all the way to the CEO—is using THEIR OWN money to hire you. And at the end of the day, your salary is simply another number in their system.

Remember when I wrote that I'm going to show you the exact path to land your DREAM JOB, get PAID MORE to do it, and take COMMAND of your CAREER? Well, so many job seekers who don't go through my system let FEAR hold them back from ever fulfilling that second goal (getting PAID MORE), and therefore are blocked from reaching the third goal (taking COMMAND of their CAREER).

Using my framework, you will figure out how to confidently get PAID MORE for your dream job by negotiating your salary before accepting the offer. The first step in this journey is to understand Pay Grades and Pay Scales.

LEARNING WHAT YOU'RE WORTH

Most companies use what's called a Pay Grade System to categorize and manage the compensation levels for different job positions within the company. Pay Grades are given a label or number, and they're mapped to positions of the same level across the organization—hence the term, "That's above my Pay Grade."

When a company breaks down their Pay Grades even further, they link them to Pay Scales—which are the minimum, midpoint, and maximum annual salaries within a specific Pay Grade.

In the following example, I've listed 8 Pay Grades, each with 3 dollar amounts that correspond to the minimum salary, midpoint salary, and a maximum salary.

- Pay Grade 1: Administrative Assistant: $30,000 / $35,000 / $40,000.

- Pay Grade 2: Customer Service Representative: $28,000 / $32,000 / $36,000.

- Pay Grade 3: Marketing Specialist: $45,000 / $55,000 / $65,000.

- Pay Grade 4: Project Manager: $55,000 / $65,000 / $75,000.

- Pay Grade 5: Senior Software Engineer: $80,000 / $100,000 / $120,000.

- Pay Grade 6: Director of Sales: $100,000 / $125,000 / $150,000.

- Pay Grade 7: Chief Financial Officer: $150,000 / $200,000 / $250,000.

- Pay Grade 8: Chief Executive Officer: $200,000 / $350,000 / $500,000.

In almost all cases, your initial offer is a starting point AT OR BELOW the MIDPOINT within your Pay Scale. For instance, in the above example, someone up for the Director of Sales position would commonly be offered $120,000, which is less than the midpoint.

Companies do this because they intentionally leave space in their budget for you to counter. Their goal is to keep you as LOW on their Pay Scale as possible because it SAVES them money.

Your mission should be to figure out WHERE you sit within a particular Pay Scale and then provide an appropriate counter-offer.

When you respectfully request more, you won't risk the offer being rescinded. That only happens if you offend the company and are unreasonable in the counter-offer negotiations, which might, for instance, include you asking for a salary that's way higher than the company's Pay Scale.

By the end of this book, you'll have CLARITY on how to position yourself as the strongest candidate for your target positions. My system will show you how to find your EXACT MARKET VALUE and use your leverage to calculate a counter-offer that RAISES your salary without risking the job.

CAREER COMMANDER ASSIGNMENTS

As I mentioned earlier, at the end of each chapter I've included exercises for you to immediately implement for RESULTS. I've written these so they help you absorb the lessons from each chapter. Complete these Career Commander Assignments successfully, and they'll pay dividends from now onward in your job search process.

Don't skip this section. Nothing good in life ever comes from doing nothing. Remember, you need to commit to investing in yourself and putting in the necessary effort to create the results.

Doing the exercises for this chapter—and similar ones at the end of other chapters—will set you up for landing your dream job, getting paid more for it, and taking command of your career, all without suffering through countless applications and constant rejection.

Before you start, please know that I have PDF versions of the following exercises. To download them, simply visit CareerCommanders.com, and download the "Career Commander Assignments."

THE JOB SEARCH MYTH BUSTERS EXERCISE

This chapter's first exercise is the **Job Search Myth Busters Exercise**.

For each MYTH I debunked in this chapter, rate it from 1 (low) to 10 (high) on how much it has affected you and your job search up to this point.

Myth 1: It will take you months to find a job.

How strongly has this myth affected your previous job searches?

(Low) 1 - 2 - 3 - 4 - 5 - 6 - 7 - 8 - 9- 10 (High)

Myth 2: You can mass-apply with one excellent resume.

How strongly has this myth affected your previous job searches?

(Low) 1 - 2 - 3 - 4 - 5 - 6 - 7 - 8 - 9- 10 (High)

Myth 3: You need to meet every job qualification to apply.

How strongly has this myth affected your previous job searches?

(Low) 1 - 2 - 3 - 4 - 5 - 6 - 7 - 8 - 9- 10 (High)

Myth 4: To network, you need to be extroverted and well-connected.

How strongly has this myth affected your previous job searches?

(Low) 1 - 2 - 3 - 4 - 5 - 6 - 7 - 8 - 9- 10 (High)

Myth 5: Job interviews are completely out of your control.

How strongly has this myth affected your previous job searches?

(Low) 1 - 2 - 3 - 4 - 5 - 6 - 7 - 8 - 9- 10 (High)

Myth 6: The salary you're offered is non-negotiable.

How strongly has this myth affected your previous job searches?

(Low) 1 - 2 - 3 - 4 - 5 - 6 - 7 - 8 - 9- 10 (High)

THE JOB SEARCH CAREER COMMANDER EXERCISE

This chapter's second exercise is the **Job Search Career Commander Exercise**.

For each TRUTH I revealed in this chapter and have listed below, read it aloud and think about it in terms of your FUTURE job searching. Then circle "yes" if you're going to put that particular truth into action in the future (or circle "no" if you're going to ignore it).

Truth 1: I can land my dream job in days, not months.

Will you put this truth into action for your future job searches?

Yes - No

Truth 2: I need a customized resume for most of my applications.

Will you put this truth into action for your future job searches?

Yes - No

Truth 3: I don't need to be the most qualified candidate to land my dream job.

Will you put this truth into action for your future job searches?

Yes - No

Truth 4: I can become a master networker from behind my own computer screen.

Will you put this truth into action for your future job searches?

Yes - No

Truth 5: When preparing for job interviews, I can gain control when I know how to answer any question I'm asked.

Will you put this truth into action for your future job searches?

Yes - No

Truth 6: I will negotiate my salary before accepting a job offer.

Will you put this truth into action for your future job searches?

Yes - No

THE MYTH BUSTERS AND CAREER COMMANDER STATEMENT

The next exercise relates to what I call the **Myth Busters And Career Commander Statemen**t. I want you to apply this statement to yourself in one of several ways.

You could type out the following statement, add your name in the right spot, add the right myth in the right spot, and then print and sign the statement.

Or you could record a video of yourself saying the following statement into the camera, and of course just add your name and the myth into the appropriate spots.

Or you can log on to our Career Commanders Community (access below) and complete your statement there.

Here's the statement:

I [NAME], am committed to stepping into the New Way of Job Searching where I am going to put the power back in my hands. Today, I let go of the Old Way and its Myths that have held me back and embrace a path of truth and action.

I recognize that the [NAME OF MYTH(S)] has influenced my job search, but it's not going to any longer! I am ready to break free of this myth and move forward with confidence, knowledge, and a supportive community behind me. It's time to become a Career Commander!

THE CAREER COMMANDERS COMMUNITY

Along with people just like you, I have created a joint online Facebook and LinkedIn community called CAREER COMMANDERS.

As a reader of this book, you're not required to join us. But, wow, I seriously urge you to join our community.

To join our community of like-minded people who are taking COMMAND of their CAREERS (and gain access to some pretty awesome job opportunities), visit CareerCommanders.com and join our Career Commanders Facebook and LinkedIn groups.

CHAPTER 2: THE DREAM JOB FORMULA

In this chapter, you're going to discover the HIDDEN PITFALL that causes mainstream job search tactics to FAIL and learn my DREAM JOB FORMULA that eliminates the wasted time and guesswork in your job search process for GOOD.

The DREAM JOB FORMULA is my proprietary framework that has helped thousands of job seekers just like you land the job they desire and deserve by transforming them into the OBVIOUS CANDIDATE.

Then we'll go through the following CAREER COMMANDER ASSIGNMENTS, all of which will transform you into the OBVIOUS CANDIDATE, where you'll:

- Identify your EXACT dream job.

- Uncover all the different versions of your dream occupation's JOB TITLE so you can find all opportunities with those JOB TITLES.

- Use the two FRAMING HACKS to become the obvious candidate, regardless of your qualifications or experience.

- Find your specific NICHE to eliminate your competition.

Are you ready to separate yourself from 99% of all other candidates?

COMMIT TO YOURSELF AND GET IN THE GAME

Like every chapter in this book, I urge you to take this chapter seriously.

Don't just flick through these pages like how we sometimes scroll through social media posts on our phones.

Don't just read the first paragraph of each section like how we sometimes just read the first paragraph of news articles.

Remember, there's a difference between being a spectator and a participant. Spectators like to watch, but never actually get in the game. And as a result, they don't reap the rewards.

So get in the game and be a participant! That's how you're going to go from merely WANTING your dream job to ACTUALLY LANDING your dream job.

THE HIDDEN PITFALL THAT CAUSES MAINSTREAM JOB SEARCH TACTICS TO FAIL AND HOW YOU CAN BEAT IT

In this chapter, I'll expose the hidden PITFALL that causes mainstream job search tactics to fail, and I'll also show how you can beat it using The Dream Job Formula.

When I first started helping job seekers, I couldn't understand why my methods weren't consistently working. I often got excellent results for my clients, but not all the time. So, as I explored in previous chapters, I tore everything down and started over from scratch. And that's when I uncovered a PITFALL that changed EVERYTHING.

Remember, The OLD WAY of job searching is BROKEN and it works AGAINST people like you. The OLD WAY involved people —including your friends and loved ones—who faced limited prospects for advancing above their current position, who wanted to find a more fulfilling job, or who were unexpectedly fired.

They'd spend countless hours STUCK in their job search. They'd constantly rewrite their resume, not knowing what phrases did or didn't grab the attention of recruiters. They'd endlessly apply for positions where they knew they could work, but deep down knew it was a role that wouldn't fulfill them. They'd endure all forms of rejection, including impersonal email rejections, hiring managers "ghosting" them, and never receiving any feedback after interviews.

As a result, both their professional and personal lives would take a massive hit. They'd spiral into an abyss of doubt and frustration. Their confidence shattered, they'd struggle to see a way out of the cycle of rejection and disappointment. The promising careers they once envisioned seemed like an unattainable dream.

MEET ERIC

Eric was one of those people. A brilliant guy with a background in Product Engineering, Eric excelled as one of the lead Product Engineers at his previous company. However, when it came to navigating the job market to find a new position, he found himself at a loss. Despite his expertise in designing and creating awesome products that sell, he struggled with marketing and selling himself effectively in his job search.

The reality is, like many others, Eric was thrust into his job search without a clear starting point, leaving a significant gap in his process. This lack of direction made it difficult for him to make progress, despite all of his research and the guidance he sought online.

YOU'RE NOT ALONE

I want you to know that, if you're stuck in your job search like Eric and millions of others who aren't in command of their career, you're NOT alone. In fact, according to Randstad USA, which is a multi-billion dollar recruiting company that specializes in OUT-DATED ways of job searching, American job seekers take on average 5 MONTHS to land a new position. And of course, that's what happens—because the average American job seeker is using inefficient techniques that HAVEN'T worked for years and STILL DON'T work.

Plus, around 82% of job seekers say that searching for a new job is stressful because of all the pressure to secure employment, uncertainty about the future, and the competitive nature of the job market.

Also, just to be clear, these two figures relate to people ACTIVELY searching for jobs. They don't even take into account people who are in jobs they can't stand and want to explore other opportunities but don't know where to start.

Just consider the following statistics. According to Gallup's 2022 report, "State of the Global Workplace," in the US:

- 50% of workers are stressed.

- 41% of workers are worried.

- 22% of workers are sad.

- 18% of workers are angry.

All of this relates to the biggest PITFALL that causes mainstream job search techniques to fail, which is how they treat the job search process as a fragmented puzzle instead of a unified, interconnected system that's built on the right foundation—which I'll show you here shortly.

MEET RACHEL

But first I want to tell you about my friend Rachel, who got a job at a great company after college and had been working her way up the organization for 6 years. Everything was going great—until she was unexpectedly laid off.

When she reached out to me, I could see how stressed and desperate she was. But it wasn't solely because she had lost her job and then spent six weeks searching for jobs which resulted in NO interviews—she was also just over a month away from her wedding.

She told me how she had spent hours every day tweaking and customizing her resume, submitting new applications, and preparing for interviews. Exasperated, she told me she wanted to find a job that appreciated her unique skills, experiences, and values. And she wanted a position that was secure and rewarding, without spending months on end searching.

But the doors just wouldn't open for her. With each rejection, she had to start all over again. Rewriting her resume, scouring job boards for new openings, and hoping that the right person would see her application. Over and over again.

That is, until I suggested that she was missing the right SYSTEM. I said, "Rachel, you're currently in the middle of what I call the JOB SEARCH CRAZY CYCLE. To get out of it, I'll give you the uniquely designed system we use to get job seekers like you back on your feet. I'll even guide you through it one-on-one until you find the job you truly desire and deserve."

So, I gave Rachel the first part of the system, and she immediately got started. Her plan was to move through it as quickly as possible with the goal of being in her new job by her wedding day.

But there was a problem, and she fell into the HIDDEN PITFALL. This is the trap many job seekers fall into even after they're shown the RIGHT way. You see, Rachel was still under the false impression that her job search was split up into several different individual parts, including:

- Building her resume and LinkedIn profile.

- Applying for jobs.

- Networking.

- Preparing for interviews.

And as a result, she thought she could skip around and do it even quicker. She went back to watching YouTube videos, reading blog posts, and trying the best "job application secrets" when applying for open positions.

The problem was, when one part of her process failed—whether it was her resume, applying for jobs, networking, or something else—it set EVERYTHING back to the beginning.

Fortunately for Rachel, only a week had passed since our initial meeting, and I was able to get her back on track. But she learned a very important lesson—that the norms created by the vast majority of job search advice in our society were actively damaging her career prospects because they treated the job search process as a series of fragmented, separate steps.

She also realized that the key to a customized and successful job search relied on having a profound understanding of herself and then transferring that knowledge across each phase of her search process—also known as having the RIGHT FOUNDATION.

Once Rachel got back on the right path and invested a little bit of extra time to set up the right foundation, her entire job search experience changed. In fact, she was able to take her strong work ethic and follow our system step-by-step to secure SIX interviews in just TWO weeks!

We even had to turn her job search OFF because of the amount of interest she was getting. And after she completed those interviews, she had multiple offers on the table and successfully secured a higher level AND higher paying position than her prior job.

Better yet, she accepted the position a week before her wedding with a negotiated start date right after her honeymoon. Is that awesome or what?

After learning how her job search process is entirely CONNECTED, Rachel has used her lifetime access to our system to propel her career to even further heights and has currently applied for and received two promotions within her company. This is what it's all about!

In this book, I'm going to unveil the entire system that Rachel used to take COMMAND of her CAREER. But before I do, I want to show you the backbone on which this system is based—**The DREAM JOB FORMULA**.

THE DREAM JOB FORMULA

This system is designed to be your ultimate assistant that guides you step-by-step through each part of your job search process—from gaining a deep understanding of what makes YOU unique to negotiating your FINAL SALARY when you have multiple offers on the table.

The reason this system is so successful is because it's based on my proprietary DREAM JOB FORMULA, which is:

$(AG \times R^8 + T^3) / Y =$ **Your Dream Job**

Rest assured, you won't need to know calculus to understand this formula! Here is what each component in this formula stands for.

The first element in the formula is **AG**.

AG stands for our **Actionable Guidance**. This is all of the in-depth training in this book that shows you the exact steps you need to take to find your dream job.

What makes my guidance different is that it is entirely ACTIONABLE. Out there in the Professional Recruitment Industrial Complex, the mainstream advice they dole out just highlights the pain of job searching—but never provides solutions. Unlike my system, they don't give you everything you need to succeed in your job search.

The second element in the formula is R^8.

R^8 stands for our **8 Resource Manuals**. These include resources that I've specifically designed and built to do all the hard work FOR you. These will SAVE you TIME and remove all the guesswork from the equation.

I believe that wasted time is wasted money. That's why each of my resource manuals is simple to use and expedites the most time-consuming parts of your job search process.

The third element in the formula is **T³**.

T³ stands for my **3 Exclusive, Corporate-Level Tools** that will immediately put the power back into your hands.

These aren't low-impact tools. These are the GAME-CHANGERS that will change your job search. Until now, these kinds of tools have only been available to the highest-level executives who are going through corporate-sponsored programs that cost $10,000 or more. But I've made them directly available to YOU as part of my system because they are too important NOT to include.

Remember how I wrote about how The OLD WAY of job searching was built for the COMPANIES, NOT for you and other job seekers? Well, that's the case because companies use tools that do all the work for them to FIND candidates like you—and by giving them to you, I'm essentially providing you with a CHEAT CODE that will shorten your job search to just DAYS instead of MONTHS.

The fourth element in the formula is **Y**.

Y stands for the most important part of all—**YOU**.

The DREAM JOB FORMULA doesn't work without You. I didn't include "You" in my formula to make it appear custom or to say that its results are based on your current skills and experiences. No. Your DNA and how you position yourself goes MUCH deeper—and it refers to the science of becoming what I call the OBVIOUS CANDIDATE to the key decision-makers who will HIRE you for your dream job.

HOW CAN YOU BECOME THE OBVIOUS CANDIDATE?

It's actually a lot simpler than you think—but almost NO ONE out there in the current job market does it the right way.

Think of it this way: You have one main mission in your job search—to land your dream job. Right? But if you haven't landed your dream job yet, that's pretty compelling evidence that there's something lacking with your previous approach to job searches. Agreed?

So why is that? It's quite possible that you've been focusing on the wrong person. You might have thought that you should focus on becoming who YOU think you need to be to look good to your target companies. That is, you've probably been focusing on YOURSELF.

However, that's missing the most important point. It's NOT about YOU. And it's certainly NOT about how you think you're looking to others from YOUR perspective.

Instead, the focus should be almost entirely on the WANTS and NEEDS of your AUDIENCES—the DECISION-MAKERS reading your resume, filtering your application, and taking you through the interview process.

Back when I was job searching, I didn't take the time to think about who my AUDIENCES were. Therefore, I didn't understand their pain points, let alone how I could customize my resume, LinkedIn, interviews, and other parts of my job search to provide SOLUTIONS to each of their PROBLEMS. Does that sound familiar? Does that maybe even resonate with you because it's what you've also done in the past?

I wasn't the only one guilty of this. Almost every single job seeker who hires me is prioritizing THEMSELVES instead of their AUDIENCES. Granted, it's completely normal for people to assume that's the correct way, but it's actually backwards.

We're often our own harshest critics. Accordingly, we want to portray ourselves in the best way possible. When we're searching and applying for jobs, though, we AREN'T the one who is choosing us for the job—it's the key decision-makers, not us.

So, who are your AUDIENCES? And what do you need to do to become the OBVIOUS CANDIDATE in their eyes?

Importantly, this doesn't involve changing who you are or embellishing your past. All that's required is knowing WHAT each key decision-maker is looking for, and HOW you can communicate your own unique skills, experiences, and values in a way that grabs their attention.

Up to this point, I've mentioned the key decision-makers several times. Now it's time to dive deep into WHO they are so that you can become the OBVIOUS CANDIDATE.

THE 4 KEY DECISION-MAKERS

There are four key decision-makers in the job search and hiring process. Three are human and one is not—and you need to HOOK all of them to land your dream job. They are:

- The recruiter.

- The Applicant Tracking System (ATS).

- The interviewer.

- The hiring manager.

DECISION-MAKER 1: THE RECRUITER

The first key decision-maker is the recruiter. This could be a recruiter who works in your target company's Human Resources Department. Or it could be a recruiter from an agency who has been hired by your target company.

Until recently, recruiters were tasked with manually searching through hundreds or thousands of candidates a day—especially if they worked for a large company. They used to look through each resume and application one-by-one. These days, they rarely ever look at a resume sent to them until they first check the LinkedIn Recruiter tool.

Recruiters in almost every industry pay big money to use this tool. At the time of writing this book, one LinkedIn Recruiter account for just one year costs $10,800!

Recruiters use this tool to find the best candidates for an open position with just a few clicks. In a way, the tool is similar to Google in that it searches vast amounts of information (LinkedIn's database), and shows you the results. But with LinkedIn Recruiter, a recruiter can segment and filter their search results in numerous ways, all of which helps them find prospects (you) who meet their criteria.

LinkedIn Recruiter makes the lives of recruiters drastically easier, and it provides them with a shortcut to finding the right candidate. However, it has been bad news for most job seekers because if they don't know how to position themselves with certain keywords in their LinkedIn PROFILE, they will NEVER get seen.

But don't worry. While it's BAD news for most job seekers, it's going to turn into one of your greatest ADVANTAGES. We'll explore this in more depth when we get to chapter 4, where I'll show you how to stand out on the first page of LinkedIn Recruiter for your dream job. But I'll share the first—and most important—step with you right now. You see, there's one common thing searched for by EVERY recruiter—it is the JOB TITLE. And to show up in their search results, you need to have that job title in the HEADLINE of your LinkedIn profile.

Yes, this sounds simple, but most job seekers don't do it—and as a result, never give themselves the opportunity to get noticed by their most prominent key decision-maker.

I know that you might be thinking: "Tommy, what if I've never held the JOB TITLE of my Dream Job? How can I still show up on the first page of LinkedIn Recruiter?"

For example, if your dream job is to be an Artificial Intelligence Ethicist, you might be thinking, "How can I show up in the first page of results for a recruiter searching for Artificial Intelligence Ethicists on LinkedIn if I haven't yet been an Artificial Intelligence Ethicist?"

It'll be ok! In our exercise at the end of this chapter, I'll show you the two FRAMING HACKS you can use to include ANY job title in your LinkedIn HEADLINE—no matter if you've done it or not and without being untruthful.

DECISION-MAKER 2: THE APPLICANT TRACKING SYSTEM (ATS)

The second key decision-maker isn't a person at all. It's the Applicant Tracking System, or ATS for short.

I'm curious, have you ever been in a situation where you thought you were a shoo-in for an interview, yet after sending in your resume, never received an invite?

The culprit was probably the Applicant Tracking System.

Today, almost every company uses ATS software to filter the resumes of applicants. They do this by checking if the resumes correspond to the keywords contained in their posted job description. Which means that even if you're the most qualified person for the job, your resume will automatically be put in the "No" pile—and never be seen by other key decision-makers—if it doesn't contain the number of keywords needed to obtain a certain match rate.

Understanding this is arguably the MOST important part of your job search. In my system, I show you how you can make small changes to your base resume to beat the ATS and drastically increase your chances of making it into the final round of candidates. And even better—I automate the whole process FOR you, making it extremely simple.

Importantly, the very first thing the ATS is looking for is the SAME thing as recruiters—your job title. Not your previous job titles—but the one you have front and center on your resume.

Companies want someone who is an EXACT match to the job they're looking to fill—and they set their tools to filter for those who SAY they're the EXACT match.

DECISION-MAKER 3: THE INTERVIEWER

The third key decision-maker is the interviewer.

The most important thing the interviewer will look for is for you to back up the claims you made on your resume and LinkedIn profile.

Remember, it rarely matters if you've done the job for which you're currently applying or not. This will make a lot more sense when you get to the section below about FRAMING HACKS. But for now, rest assured that I am NOT asking you to lie.

DECISION-MAKER 4: THE HIRING MANAGER

The fourth and final key decision-maker is the hiring manager.

The hiring manager is usually the last person to look at your resume, either during or after your interview. Their goal is the same goal as the interviewer—ensuring that you can back up the claims on your resume and LinkedIn profile, and then seeing how you fit into their existing team.

Once again, by simply FRAMING yourself as the OBVIOUS Candidate and tying in your past experiences to make them RELEVANT to your dream job, you're going to place yourself as the obvious choice over other candidates who aren't doing the same.

Remember, the science behind becoming the Obvious Candidate starts with WHO YOU ARE in the eyes of your key decision-makers—not who you are to YOURSELF.

CAREER COMMANDER ASSIGNMENT: BECOMING THE OBVIOUS CANDIDATE

In this exercise, you'll uncover how to become the OBVIOUS CANDIDATE for your DREAM JOB.

This exercise has 5 steps, so I want you to get out a good old-fashioned printed notebook, or open a doc on your computer. That way you can write down your findings and answers to each exercise.

Better yet, you can download a PDF of the following by visiting CareerCommanders.com.

STEP 1: DECLARE YOUR DREAM JOB

Earlier in this chapter, you learned that your key decision-makers prioritize one thing above everything else—the JOB TITLE on their job posting and whether it matches with the JOB TITLE on your resume or on your LinkedIn.

There's no way you can become the OBVIOUS CANDIDATE if you don't know the exact dream job you're looking to land.

So, the first step is to DECLARE your DREAM JOB.

This actually doesn't have to be a specific job, such as one tied to an actual job posting or specific company. Instead, this is the job title that you REALLY want.

Here are some entry-level and mid-level examples:

- Business Development Intern.
- Financial Analyst.
- Marketing Manager.
- Social Media Manager.
- Software Developer.
- Operations Director.

And don't forget the C-Suite! Here are some C-Suite job titles:

- Chief Executive Officer (CEO).
- Chief Marketing Officer (CMO).
- Chief Sustainability Officer (CSO).
- Chief Technology Officer (CTO).

Whatever it is for YOU, I want you to DECLARE your DREAM JOB TITLE by writing it down.

STEP 2: FIND ALL THE TITLES OF YOUR DREAM JOB

Next, once you have your dream job written down, it's crucial to find all of the SYNONYMS—or ALTERNATIVE TITLES—of your dream job. You see, while your dream job doesn't change, the TITLE of it DOES from company to company, industry to industry, or region to region.

An example that relates to COMPANIES: Amazon might regularly use the job title Product Marketing Manager, whereas Apple might frequently use the job title Content Marketing Manager, but in essence the two jobs are more or less the same.

An example that relates to INDUSTRIES: The construction industry might frequently use the job title Business Intelligence Analyst, whereas the healthcare industry might more commonly use the job title Strategic Planning Analyst, but fundamentally the two jobs are more or less identical.

An example that relates to REGIONS: In some regions, the job title for the areas of UX (which stands for user experience) might be different. For some regions, the job title UX Designer might be common, whereas in other regions, the job title UX Architect might be more prevalent, but at their core, the two jobs are the same in terms of tasks and responsibilities.

So remember, there are almost certainly various JOB TITLES that accurately describe your DREAM JOB. It's just that you've perhaps never thought of your dream job in those terms.

Luckily, there is a very easy way to find SYNONYMS of your DREAM JOB TITLE. You can do this using a feature on Google that is sometimes called "Google for Jobs" and sometimes called "Google Search for Jobs."

Finding this job tool isn't intuitive. For instance, there isn't a single URL that I can tell you to type in that will take you directly to the right page.

But it's easy to find this feature if you simply type "jobs near me" into the Google search bar. After you search for that generic term, a large title named "Jobs" will show up at the top of the screen. This is Google showing you what it thinks are the best jobs for you that are located near you.

After that short list of jobs, there will be a link that says, "100+ more jobs." Click that—or the mapped button to enter the feature—and you'll be taken to a new page that is essentially the "Google for Jobs" / "Google Search for Jobs" tool.

When you're on that main page, type in your DREAM JOB TITLE. For this chapter, I'll assume you've entered "Marketing Specialist."

On that Google results page, you'll be able to refine your job search according to the following filters (which vary depending on various factors):

- Location.

- Date posted (which means that date a recruiter or company published the job posting).

- Requirements.

- Remote.

- Type (which means type of job).

- Experience Level (no degree, bachelor's degree, etc.)

- Company type.

On that page, pay particular attention to the variety of listed Titles in the job postings.

When you search through the opportunities, Google will list a bunch of roles with job titles that are similar to the one you typed in. For instance, if you initially typed in "Marketing Specialist," then scrolled through the opportunities, Google could show you the following suggested job titles:

- Marketing Coordinator.

- Marketing Manager.

- Marketing Analyst.

They could also show you "Titles" such as the following, which perhaps aren't technically job titles, but are still nonetheless used by recruiters in the main headings of their posted jobs:

- Media Marketing.

- Digital Marketing.

- Email Marketing.

These ALTERNATIVE JOB TITLES all somehow relate to your DREAM JOB. These aren't just suggestions, these are the actual posted title variations from all the job postings that Google has found.

But importantly, not all of the listed titles will have a meaningful connection with YOU and your DREAM JOB. For instance, the following titles are also listed by Google, but you might decide that they're IRRELEVANT to you:

- Marketing Professor.

- Technical Marketer.

So, for this part of your CAREER COMMANDER ASSIGNMENT, go into Google and identify the most RELEVANT TITLES of your DREAM JOB. Then, write them all down on your CAREER COMMANDER sheet.

STEP 3: FRAMING HACKS

You're probably wondering how this works if you've never held the EXACT title of your dream job. You're also possibly wondering how you can make this work without feeling like you're lying to decision-makers. You can achieve this by using one or both of the following two FRAMING HACKS.

The first FRAMING HACK is called the TARGETED APPROACH. This is where you can simply include your current or most relevant prior title, and then add a word like "Aspiring" or "Future" in front of the TITLE of your DREAM JOB.

For example, if you're currently a Marketing Representative, and your dream job is to be an Operations Manager, you could simply state your title as "Marketing Representative & Aspiring Operations Manager."

Or, if you're currently a Medical Receptionist who is sick of answering phones all day, and your dream job involves working in the lab, you could simply state your title as "Medical Receptionist & Future Medical Laboratory Technician."

Here are some additional examples:

- Attorney & Aspiring Web Designer.

- Urban Planner & Aspiring Chef.

- Elderly Care Coordinator & Future Film Editor.

- Customer Support Specialist & Future Crisis Communications Specialist.

This is called the targeted approach because it targets the exact dream job you want.

This approach is best used in the HEADLINE of your LinkedIn profile. Here's why: LinkedIn Recruiter's algorithm ignores qualifying words such as "Aspiring" or "Future." Instead, the job title itself is the only thing this software tool craves—and it's also the key piece of information that will appear in BOLD to the recruiters using LinkedIn Recruiter who are searching for candidates who have your exact TITLE.

By the way, if you're looking for inspiration about how some job seekers are already using this approach, type "Aspiring" into LinkedIn's search, and you'll see examples of people who have figured out this hack.

The second FRAMING HACK is called the OVERARCHING APPROACH. This approach is what you should use in your resume and in your job interviews.

This requires taking your dream job and slightly generalizing it based on the theme of its job title and your experience level.

For example, if you want to be a Client Relationship Manager, yet don't have any executive-level experience from your past work history, then you could generalize the "Client Relationship" part of the job title and instead say "Client Relations."

Then, you could simply include the word "Professional" at the end to portray ample experience. So, if you haven't yet held the job, instead of saying "Client Relationship Manager" you could say "Client Relations Professional."

This allows you the flexibility to FRAME your relevant professional experience around "Client Relations" whether or not you've actually been in that role.

Here's one more example. Say your goal is to work as a Financial Analyst, but you lack extensive experience. Well, you could FRAME yourself as a Financial Consultant and highlight your analytical skills and how they relate to providing valuable financial advice.

You see, there are similarities across every job, and you can pull relevant experience from anything—even if it seems unrelated.

One more thing. If you do have executive-level experience anywhere in your past, it's important to replace the word "Professional" with "Executive." So, instead of saying "Client Relations Professional" you would say "Client Relations Executive."

You have the relevant experience to back it up—even if it was in a different job—and you should showcase it to your key decision-makers.

As part of your CAREER COMMANDER ASSIGNMENT for this chapter, now is the time to implement these two framing hacks.

Specifically, using the TARGETED APPROACH, write down your new LinkedIn heading in the following format: [Current Job Title] & Aspiring/Future [Dream Job Title].

(A quick note: If you've already worked at your dream job, then you can skip the previous exercise and the following exercise. For instance, if you're currently an Interior Designer and that's ALSO your dream job, then you obviously wouldn't need to have the following as your LinkedIn headline: Interior Designer & Aspiring Interior Designer!)

Next, using the OVERARCHING APPROACH, jot down some notes about how you can frame your experience more broadly so that you can include this general information both in your resume and in your job interviews. This is also the Dream Job Title you will use for your Obvious Candidate Statement at the end of this assignment.

STEP 4: NICHING DOWN

This step is "Application-specific" UNLESS your Dream Job only applies to a specific industry. Now, if you've heard the term "Niche" before, but aren't sure exactly what it means, think of it as declaring your specialty.

For instance, if you really wanted New York Style Pizza, would you choose Pizza Hut, Domino's Pizza, or Frank's New York Pizza? You'd obviously pick Frank's because it says "New York" right there in its name.

Just as many businesses include their exact SPECIALTY in their title—otherwise known as their NICHE—you can do the same thing in your HEADLINE.

In fact, it puts you in a whole new class of candidates—as you're showcasing yourself as a professional who not only does the EXACT job your key decision-makers are looking for, but also does it in their EXACT industry.

This drastically shrinks your competition. And you can use this NICHING strategy for each one of your job applications.

All you need to do is include the INDUSTRY of the company where you're applying.

You've already set yourself up perfectly to pull relevance from your past experiences with a forward-looking Headline—that being one that portrays future opportunity—and you can do this with INDUSTRY, as well—whether you've worked in the industry, or not.

Companies care about the future more than the past. They want candidates who are naturally interested in their industry. And this one simple tweak will have them placing you at the very top of their list.

STEP 5: CREATE YOUR OBVIOUS CANDIDATE STATEMENT

Here are some examples of Obvious Candidate Statements:

- Client Relations Professional with a special focus in the Energy sector.

- Account Manager specializing in the Tourism field.

- Sales Representative with a particular emphasis on the Healthcare industry.

So, for this CAREER COMMANDER ASSIGNMENT, it's time for you to create your own OBVIOUS CANDIDATE STATEMENT. Use the following as a guide:

- [Dream Job Title] with a special focus in the [Industry].

If your dream job spans multiple industries, and you'd be ok with working in two or more of those industries, then you can have two or more versions of your statement. Just have a statement for each industry. For example, if your dream job is to be a Software Engineer, and you'd be fine with working in the Entertainment or Education industries (but not, say, the Construction or Food industries), then you could write the following OBVIOUS CANDIDATE STATEMENT into some of your job applications:

- Software Engineer with a special focus in the Entertainment industry.

And you'd write the following version of your OBVIOUS CANDIDATE STATEMENT into some of your other job applications:

- Software Engineer with a special focus in the Education industry.

The OBVIOUS CANDIDATE STATEMENT is your public declaration of how you're going to position yourself throughout your job search and land your dream job, and I'd highly recommend creating one for the TARGETED APPROACH (to be used on your LinkedIn Profile) and the OVERARCHING APPROACH (to be used on your resume)

SHARE YOUR OBVIOUS CANDIDATE STATEMENT WITH THE CAREER COMMANDER COMMUNITY

As I mentioned in my previous chapter, we've created a CAREER COMMANDERS COMMUNITY of like-minded job seekers just like you.

Remember that even though you're reading this book and perhaps haven't yet signed up for one of the programs I offer through Job Seekers University—or our game-changing Done-for-You Job Search service—you're still welcome to join my Career Commanders Community.

There are professionals with all types of different backgrounds within our community, some of whom are key decision-makers looking for someone just like YOU. That's why I'd STRONGLY encourage you to join our community. You never know who's looking for you on the other side!

To join our community of like-minded people who are taking COMMAND of their CAREERS, visit CareerCommanders.com and become a member of our Facebook and LinkedIn groups.

CHAPTER 3: GET THE UNFAIR ADVANTAGE

In this chapter, I'll show you how to get the UNFAIR ADVANTAGE in your job search! We'll also explore why—contrary to popular opinion—you actually DON'T need to be the most QUALIFIED or EXPERIENCED candidate to land your dream job!

First, I'm going to reveal the psychology behind HOW your key decision-makers choose the right candidate for the job.

Next, I'll show you how to take advantage of this psychology and use the number one marketing tool in your job search arsenal to become the MOST Obvious Candidate.

Lastly, I'll give you the writing guide and framework you need to easily HOOK the key decision-makers at your top opportunities and make them eager to learn more.

After reading this chapter, you'll gain **clarity** on how to MARKET and SELL yourself and go from the Obvious Candidate to the MOST OBVIOUS CANDIDATE.

THE BIG QUESTION

Have you ever come across a job posting that seems like a perfect fit, only to have your hopes shattered when you see the required qualifications and experience? If you have, then you've fallen victim to the number ONE thing that holds millions of job seekers back from landing their dream jobs every year—thinking they need to meet all qualifications in a job posting to apply.

Here's the truth. You DON'T need to be an EXPERT in your field, or even the most qualified candidate, to land your dream job.

I acknowledge you might be thinking, "Tommy, why don't I need to be the most qualified candidate? Don't companies hire the candidate with the most experience or best accomplishments?"

During my own job search, I used to freak out about those exact questions. I thought that, logically, of course recruiters and hiring managers must prefer the most experienced and qualified candidates.

However, after analyzing the hiring processes of numerous employers, I've realized that those assumptions just aren't accurate. Worse still, they unnecessarily block countless job seekers from applying for the jobs they truly desire and deserve.

The reason for this reality is best stated by Zig Ziglar, one of the most successful authors and salesmen of all time, who once wrote:

*"People don't **buy** for **logical** reasons. They **buy** for **emotional** reasons."*

(I **bolded** those letters, not Ziglar. The **bolding** will make sense as you read onward.)

Think about it. When a company is selling a product or service, they're focused on gaining a profound understanding of their audiences and then marketing it with the backbone STORY to positively impact the perception of their customers—which in turn, makes the product or service the OBVIOUS choice.

This is why any product or service—no matter how good or bad it objectively is—can outsell and outcompete the BEST products and services in the industry if they have the RIGHT marketing.

However, while Ziglar's statement perfectly reflects the reality of buying products and services, it doesn't exactly capture the essence of the job search and hiring process. So here's my slightly updated version of Ziglar's words:

*"People don't **hire** for **logical** reasons. They **hire** for **emotional** reasons."*

And now here's my full-fledged version, which I've written in first-person to help you internalize this truth:

*"When I apply for my dream job, **logical** reasoning won't be the number one determinant key decision-makers use to **hire** me. Instead, they will prioritize **hiring** me based on their own **emotional** reasons."*

FLIPPING BURGERS, RAKING IN BILLIONS

As an example, look at McDonald's. We all know that Mickey D's doesn't have the best quality food. Near my home, I can find several other restaurants that have higher-quality and better-tasting food. You probably can, too.

So, how then did McDonald's earn $35 billion in the US in 2023? Put in another way, how does McDonald's outshine everyone else in sales?

It's because the key decision-makers at the Golden Arches have a profound understanding of their audience and know how to market and sell themselves to that audience.

This EXACT same thing can happen in your job search. And before you think I'm comparing you to McDonald's—I'm not. The unique skills, experiences, and values you possess make you a MUCH more valuable prospect!

But, my point is that in a crowded field of competitors, you too can stand out against your competition, just like McDonald's stands out against its competition.

OLIVER'S STORY

I talked recently with a buddy of mine, who I'll call Oliver. Before he completed my 5-step Obvious Candidate framework a few years ago, Oliver would regularly think things like: "I can't apply for the jobs I really want because there will be a ton of other applicants who are WAY more qualified than me. I just wouldn't stand a chance."

Oliver was trapped in a cycle of self-doubt and fear of rejection that held him back from pursuing the jobs he truly desired and deserved.

After he implemented my job search formula and system, he told me: "I love the fact that people don't need to be the most qualified or have the highest level of experience or expertise."

Using my system, Oliver learned how to market and sell himself the RIGHT way in his job search process. The result? He applied for jobs that he was certain would be given to other candidates who had more experience and qualifications than he did, but he didn't let that stop him. And in a short time, Oliver landed a job he NEVER thought he would get—a job that paid him $20,000 MORE than his previous one!

JOHN'S STORY

Now I'd like to share with you a story of a client of mine, John.

John had spent over 7 years working in education and athletics for a church. But after he and his wife decided to start a family, they knew they wanted to move away from where they were currently living and move back to their hometown to be closer to their extended family.

To achieve that, John knew he was going to have to leave his career in Ministry behind. Also, he knew he wanted to get a job in Client Relations. So to prepare, John got his Master's Degree in Organizational Leadership.

But his degree wasn't enough to get him a job. The problem was, he didn't know how to write an engaging resume, and he was sure that his lack of qualifications and experience were his own worst enemies.

Imagine the feeling. He had just moved his family. He had no idea how he would ever successfully make this career shift, and a massive part of his frustration was his wrong assumptions that he was at a strategic disadvantage over other competing job candidates.

In preparing for his career shift, for years John had mastered skills that would help him as a Client Relationship Professional, and he knew deep down that, even though the industry was different, he would be a great fit in Client Relations.

He just had no idea how to communicate those skills and experiences in a way that would be thought of as "on par" or even "better than" a candidate who had a background that made them appear to be more qualified.

That's when he started to do some research, found me online, and hired me to help him land his dream job.

As he worked with me, I explained how the key to his success and beating other candidates was through HOW he would MARKET and SELL himself—NOT how qualified he might appear on paper.

I also explained how EVERY job seeker, regardless of their expertise, needs a customized sales and marketing strategy to become not just the Obvious Candidate, but the MOST Obvious Candidate.

Gradually, John started switching his mindset, and his plan was to learn how to build his personal brand and communicate his unique skills and accomplishments in a way that would make him the most attractive choice for Client Relationship positions.

But there were two FALSE beliefs that held him back:

- He still believed that he was an "extreme case" and that my system wouldn't work because of his lack of relevant qualifications or experience.

- He still believed that, no matter what he did, his past failures would prevent him from being successful.

But he didn't give up. Over two weeks, he put in the hard work and made the DREAM JOB FORMULA work for him, transforming him into a self-marketing machine. John did this in three ways:

- He crafted a new resume that perfectly framed each one of his experiences as relevant to his future profession.

- He updated his LinkedIn Profile so that it marketed him 24/7 as a dedicated professional focused on Client Relationships.

- He had an entire Application Process automated to send him the best opportunities every day.

All of this resulted in him being able to easily and effectively sell himself during his networking and interview processes.

Here's the best part, though—and it's one that I'm most proud of—John didn't have to change anything about himself. Here are three things he DIDN'T have to do:

- He DIDN'T have to become a Resume Writing Expert or a Professional Speaker who knew how to sell himself.

- He DIDN'T have to come up with any false truths about his background or professional history.

- He DIDN'T have to become the most qualified candidate on paper.

All he had to do was follow my step-by-step formula and system and let it do that work FOR him. John didn't have the time to become an expert in anyone other than himself. And I know you don't, either.

That's why I built my system so that it can be your guide and assistant throughout every step of your job search, making you the MOST Obvious Candidate in the MINDS of the key decision-makers who are responsible for finding and hiring you.

Because remember, people don't hire based on **logic**. They do so based on **emotion**.

Also remember that there will ALWAYS be someone more qualified than you. The key is knowing how to position yourself as the Most Obvious Candidate.

So what happened to John? Well, after going completely through our system, he applied for his dream job and beat out several other candidates —who were more qualified than him on paper—and John landed a great Client Relationship position. And while John LOVES his new career, if he wants to change in the future, he won't be afraid to put himself out there and apply for other opportunities. Why? Because now he realizes that the key to career success isn't being the most qualified or experienced—it's having a SYSTEM he can count on.

FROM THE OBVIOUS CANDIDATE TO THE MOST OBVIOUS CANDIDATE

Now, you might be thinking questions such as:

- "How can I do this for myself?"

- "How can I market and sell myself?"

- "How can I go from being the Obvious Candidate to being the MOST Obvious Candidate?"

- "How can I portray myself to key decision-makers as the MOST Obvious Candidate?"

It all starts with your HOOK—how you grab the attention of all your key decision-makers using the number one tool in your job search arsenal, which is your resume.

More specifically, it's all about the SUMMARY STATEMENT at the top of your resume—the very first impression that you'll make on your audiences.

THE HOOK OF YOUR JOB SEARCH = YOUR SUMMARY STATEMENT

Why is the summary statement in your resume so important? Also, how can it be the main thing that takes you from the Obvious Candidate to the MOST Obvious Candidate?

What you need to know is that your summary statement isn't JUST the hook for your resume, it's also the base you will use to grab attention across every key area of your job search, including:

- It's the foundation for the "About" Section of your LinkedIn Profile.

- It's how you'll introduce yourself when getting high-value networking connections.

- And it's the answer you'll give when an interviewer says to you something like, "Tell me about yourself."

In today's cut-throat job market, where hundreds of applicants are fighting for the same job, you need to find a way to immediately stand out from the crowd.

YOUR SUMMARY STATEMENT = HOW YOU STAND OUT!

The very first paragraph in your resume is your chance to shine. So make a bold impression and show your audiences that you're precisely who they WANT and NEED.

Picture this: You've just sent off your resume, and the recruiter who's in charge of finding the right fit for your dream job is scanning through the resumes of the candidates who made it through the Applicant Tracking System (ATS).

For whatever reason, they pick your resume and see your summary statement—and something stops them in their tracks. Your words capture their attention and paint a vivid picture of your unique value.

Your credentials, achievements, and experiences—regardless of your qualifications—are all effectively communicated in the EXACT way the recruiter wants to receive them, leaving no doubt that you're the perfect fit for the job.

YOU CONTROL THE IMPRESSION YOU MAKE

Situations like what I just described above happen every day in the world of a recruiter. In fact, recruiters only spend an average of 6 SECONDS on their initial scan of your resume. They see so many bad resumes each day that they CRAVE finding a candidate who solves their pain points.

Remember, it's my mission to take all the guesswork OUT of the equation for you. And even though you can't read a recruiter's mind or get notified as soon as they read your resume, you CAN control the impression your resume leaves on them, especially the FIRST impression.

So, in a world where a single missed opportunity can mean the difference between landing your dream job and being left in the dust, a well-crafted summary statement is not just essential—it's your biggest difference-maker.

And right now, I'm going to show you how to craft your ATTENTION-GRABBING SUMMARY STATEMENT with my Hook, Line, and Summary Formula.

YOUR RESUME IS THE NUMBER ONE MARKETING TOOL IN YOUR JOB SEARCH ARSENAL

But before we begin, I want you to keep this in mind: Your resume is unlike anything else you've ever written. It's not an essay, it's not a social media post, and it's not really even an autobiography—even though it seems like it should be.

I urge you to consider your resume as being the NUMBER ONE MARKETING TOOL in your job search arsenal. And, just like how a great product will never be purchased by anyone if it doesn't have the marketing to prop it up, your resume will never stand out if it's written in a way that doesn't cater to your key decision-makers.

There's a writing style to follow. Also, there's a structure WITHIN that writing style that helps you become a self-marketing pro. And the Hook, Line, and Summary Formula is the powerful writing tool that's designed to make that a reality.

THE HOOK, LINE, AND SUMMARY FORMULA

In this section, I'll show you how to craft your attention-grabbing summary statement. To accomplish this, I'm going to break down each part of the formula, and then give you a real-life example to follow when doing this yourself.

THE 1ST PART OF THE HOOK, LINE, AND SUMMARY FORMULA

The first part of the Hook, Line, and Summary Formula relates to the following:

Action Verb(s) + Your Professional Title.

With resumes, it's extremely important to use an active voice. Unfortunately, countless job seekers use a passive voice in their resumes.

The best way to put positive, proactive emphasis on yourself is to start your most influential sentences with an Action Verb—the expression that sets up the narrative you want to create in your statement or sentence.

After picking which Action Verb best portrays you, the next step is to include your Professional Title. This is the same as the Title you uncovered in your Obvious Candidate Statement from the previous chapter.

Remember, your Professional Title doesn't have to be limited to your current or previous roles. Instead, it should exhibit a broader range of your experiences up to this point and focus on who you WANT to become.

To show how you can incorporate this in your own Summary Statement, I want to share with you Emma's story and summary statement. Emma is a client of mine who got incredible results, and I would like to show you HOW she was able to effectively hook her key decision-makers.

So, Emma hired me when she got laid-off from her Digital Marketing job, knew that she wanted to finally apply for Content Marketing Manager positions she had been dreaming about, but wasn't sure how to go about it.

Holding her back was the fact that she had never held a management position before. Because of this, she didn't know how she could stand out over other candidates who had that experience in their resumes.

So, how did I help Emma? Well, I showed her how to become the Obvious Candidate to her key decision-makers WITHOUT being untruthful.

Specifically, instead of changing her title from Digital Marketing Specialist to Content Marketing Manager, which wouldn't have been true, she changed her title to Content Marketing Professional, which was true.

This simple replacing of the word "Manager" with "Professional" was key. It gave Emma the wiggle room to maintain the integrity of WHO she was without being untruthful, and it didn't change the perception of her one bit to her key decision-makers.

Also, Emma added an action verb to the front of her title to put positive, proactive emphasis on herself, making her full title:

Accomplished Content Marketing Professional.

THE 2ND PART OF THE HOOK, LINE, AND SUMMARY FORMULA

Now let's move on to the next part of the Hook, Line, and Summary Formula. This part involves highlighting your key experiences and the total number of years you've worked in your field.

Doing this provides your key decision-makers with a sense of your background and depth of experience BEFORE they read the rest of your resume.

And if you're early on in your career, or feel like you lack the necessary length of experience required for the role, think about when you started developing the skills you need for your dream job, and use that timeframe to portray the length of your overall experience.

Here's how you can visualize this formula so far (with the new part at the end italicized and underlined):

Action Verb(s) + Professional Title _x Key Experiences_.

And here's how you can think of this formula so far:

It communicates WHO YOU ARE and WHAT YOU'VE DONE.

My client Emma had 8 years of experience in content creation. Following my formula, here is how she communicated WHO SHE IS and WHAT SHE HAS DONE. In the following, note that the *italicized and underlined* words were added during this part.

Accomplished Content Marketing Professional *with over 8 years of experience creating and optimizing compelling content across various platforms.*

THE 3RD PART OF THE HOOK, LINE, AND SUMMARY FORMULA

The third part of the formula is about highlighting your relevant specialities. Think of this as demonstrating your "field expertise." Here you'll summarize the most prevalent tasks you accomplished in your previous positions that translate well to your desired job.

With the third part added to the formula, here's how you can visualize the formula so far (with the new part at the end *italicized and underlined*):

Action Verb(s) + Professional Title x Key Experiences *x Relevant Specialties*.

And here's how you can think of this formula so far:

It communicates WHO YOU ARE, WHAT YOU'VE DONE, and WHERE YOU EXCEL.

In this part, you can write "Demonstrated history in" or "Demonstrated history of," and then you'll list your relevant specialties.

The goal is to explain your specific tasks in a way your key decision-makers want to hear them.

To show you what I mean, here's what Emma wrote using my formula. Note that the first sentence below is the same as it was previously. But the second *italicized and underlined* sentence is new.

Accomplished Content Marketing Professional with over 8 years of experience creating and optimizing compelling content across various platforms. *<u>Demonstrated history of leveraging SEO best practices, audience segmentation, and multimedia storytelling</u>*.

As you can see, Emma broke down her key experiences a step further and expanded upon exactly WHAT she did throughout her career, giving vivid examples.

I acknowledge that putting the specifics of what you've done into words can be challenging. If you're having trouble with this, I recommend finding one of your actual past job descriptions, which might give you some ideas about what to write. Alternatively, on job board sites such as *Google for Jobs* and *Indeed*, find a few current descriptions of your job, and see if they have any ideas you can use.

THE 4TH PART OF THE HOOK, LINE, AND SUMMARY FORMULA

The fourth and last part of this formula is where you'll highlight the top achievements that came from your relevant specialties and PROVE them to be true.

Now, I acknowledge that "relevant specialties" (from the previous part) and "top achievements" (from this part) might seem like the same thing. Yet while they are similar, they're actually slightly different.

Nonetheless, it's crucial to distinguish between the two. "Relevant specialties" typically refer to specific areas of expertise or skills that directly relate to the job or field, whereas "top achievements" highlight notable accomplishments or successes that showcase your abilities and track record.

With that in mind, in this part of your summary statement, really think about the results that came from your efforts in the previous part.

With the last part added to the formula, here's how you can visualize the entire formula (with the new part at the end *italicized and underlined*):

Action Verb(s) + Professional Title x Key Experiences x Relevant Specialties *x Top Achievements*.

In this part, you'll write a sentence that includes the words "resulting in," and then you'll write something about money, time, or percentages. Then you'll write about how it increased (e.g. more revenue), decreased (e.g. less time spent achieving something), or changed (e.g. a percentage increase/decrease), and then you'll connect these with your top achievements.

In other words, once you've identified the specific outcomes, do your best to show their impact by making them measurable with time, money, or percentages.

Here's how Emma did this. When reading the following, notice how Emma effectively PROVES herself and leaves no doubt that she's not just the Obvious Candidate, but the MOST Obvious Candidate to her key decision-makers. In the following, the new content is the *italicized and underlined* words added to the end.

Accomplished Content Marketing Professional with over 8 years of experience creating and optimizing compelling content across various platforms. Demonstrated history of leveraging SEO best practices, audience segmentation, and multimedia storytelling, *resulting in a 150% increase in organic traffic and tripling engagement rates on targeted campaigns*.

At this stage, some job seekers get blocked because they don't have exact numbers to communicate their top achievements.

To overcome this, consider the following two similar yet different statements, either of which Emma could have used:

- Resulting in a significant increase in organic traffic and a boost in engagement rates on targeted campaigns

- Resulting in a 150% increase in organic traffic and tripling engagement rates on targeted campaigns

To you, which statement sounds more impressive? It's the second one, right? It comes across as more significant. But why? Well, hard numbers and their impact can never be replaced.

And here's a little secret: When I started helping Emma write her summary statement, she couldn't think of any numbers to go with her results. That is, until we got more specific.

Importantly, I want you to know that you can put a number on ALMOST ANYTHING. For example, you CAN put a number on the following:

- The number of hours you saved your past company by completing a certain task early.

- The money you generated by keeping a client happy and retaining them.

- The percentage you increased engagement by leading your work team.

If you can find a number, USE it. Rough estimates are okay to use here, as long as you can back them up in your interview. And they will make your top achievements shine like GOLD over your competitors who don't have them.

ADDITIONAL EXAMPLES OF THE HOOK, LINE, AND SUMMARY FORMULA BEING USED

While my use of my real life client Emma's example above was helpful, I acknowledge it was very specific to her career and her dream job. So, here are three additional summary statements that I've written for hypothetical job seekers.

An example of a summary statement for Cameron:

Dynamic Software Engineer with 4+ years of experience designing and implementing scalable solutions for complex technical challenges. Proficient in multiple programming languages and frameworks, with extensive experience in Agile methodologies and cloud computing, resulting in reduced application response time by 50% and a 75% increase in system reliability.

An example of a summary statement for Francine:

Strategic Financial Analyst with 5+ years of experience in financial modeling, forecasting, and risk assessment in the banking sector. Skilled in analyzing market trends and developing data-driven strategies to optimize investment portfolios, resulting in $1 million in cost savings through the implementation of efficiency initiatives.

An example of a summary statement for Penelope:

Visionary Product Manager with 6+ years of experience in product lifecycle management and cross-functional team leadership. Possessing a strong background in market research, user experience design, and product development methodologies, resulting in a 200% increase in user acquisition and generating over $2 million in revenue.

An example of a summary statement for Miles:

Award-winning Creative Professional with 12+ years of experience in consumer product display design. Expertise in innovating and launching display systems, with a strong track record of targeting four emerging markets and implementing cost-cutting and streamlining processes that have contributed to over $300,000 of additional revenue.

An example of a summary statement for Clara:

Proven Certified Public Accountant with 20+ years of experience in tax planning, preparation, and compliance work. Demonstrated history of creating and operating emerging tax software to mitigate risk for a portfolio of 300 clients, saving over 30 hours and averaging a 15% increase in tax savings per client.

CAREER COMMANDER ASSIGNMENT: CREATE YOUR OWN ATTENTION-GRABBING SUMMARY STATEMENT

Your exercise for this chapter is to write your own Attention-Grabbing Summary Statement.

But first, let's recap. Here are the four parts of the formula:

- The 1st part: Action Verb(s) + Professional Title.

- The 2nd part: Key Experiences.

- The 3rd part: Relevant Specialties.

- The 4th part: Top Achievements.

Altogether, the formula is:

Action Verb(s) + Professional Title x Key Experiences x Relevant Specialties x Top Achievements.

Additionally, here are 4 templates you can use to aid your writing process:

TEMPLATE #1:

[Action Verb(s) + Desired Position] with over [#] years of experience in [Key Experiences]. Demonstrated history of [Relevant Specialties], resulting in [Top Achievements].

TEMPLATE #2:

[Action Verb(s) + Desired Position] with over [#] years of experience in [Key Experiences]. Expertise in [Relevant Specialties], with a strong track record of [Top Achievements] that have contributed to [Measurable Results].

TEMPLATE #3:

[Action Verb(s) + Desired Position] with [#]+ years of experience [Key Experiences]. Highly proficient in [Relevant Specialties]. Demonstrated history in [Top Achievements], saving over/resulting in [Measurable Results].

BONUS TEMPLATE:

For those newer to the professional world or undergoing a major career shift:

[Action Verb(s) + Desired Position] with over [#] years of training/knowledge [Key Experiences]. Skilled in [Relevant Specialties], with an established reputation of [Top Achievements], contributing to a savings/reduction/addition of [Measurable Results].

Before you start writing your own, know this: you don't have to be a natural-born writer to ace this assignment. If you methodically break down the task into the four above parts and use the provided templates, you will write an attention-grabbing resume that stands out to your key decision-makers in those crucial first 6 seconds.

Remember, what you're aiming to write is much more than just the first words your key decision-makers will see when they view your resume. Think of it as the HOOK that will draw them in and PROVE that you're precisely who they're looking for, which is how you'll go from the Obvious Candidate to the MOST Obvious Candidate in their eyes.

POST YOUR SUMMARY STATEMENT IN THE CAREER COMMANDERS COMMUNITY

As I've mentioned at the end of each chapter so far—and will continue to do so—we've created a supportive, inspiring community for job seekers just like you. Just visit CareerCommanders.com and join our Facebook and LinkedIn groups.

When you're a member, be sure to post your Summary Statement in the community!

QUESTIONS?

If you have any questions, make sure to post them in the community or email us at support@thejobseekersuniversity.com.

Also, I know you're busy being an expert in what YOU do great. If at any point you feel stuck, or don't have the time to go through the job search yourself, my team of Job Search Architects and I would love to do your job search process FOR you!

To learn more and see if we're a mutual fit, just schedule a call with us at TheJobseekersUniversity.com.

Remember to invest in yourself and play to WIN! I promise, it's the fastest path to landing the job of your dreams!

I want to end this chapter on a high. I'm going to do that by talking about Emma just one more time. So, what happened to my client? Great news: Emma got her management-level position in Content Marketing and is still working there to this day!

CHAPTER 4: BECOME INSTANTLY NOTICED

In this chapter, we'll explore the first of two Visibility Hacks that will attract recruiters and hiring managers to you like a magnet.

This chapter is the 4th step in my 5-step framework that will show you the clear path to becoming the MOST Obvious Candidate, without suffering through countless applications or facing constant rejection.

Do you remember how I previously stated that for decades the job search process has benefited the COMPANY hiring a particular candidate, rather than the actual particular candidate? And do you remember how I'm all about flipping that power dynamic so that you and other candidates can take control of your job search and career?

Well, in this chapter (where I reveal Visibility Hack #1) and the next chapter (where I reveal Visibility Hack #2), I'm going to back up those big, bold statements with clear, actionable steps you can take.

HOW CAN YOU ATTRACT RECRUITERS AND HIRING MANAGERS TO YOU LIKE A MAGNET?

The hurdle that most applicants can't jump over is the fact that COMPANIES have filters that block them from getting the job they desire and deserve. So I'm going to show you exactly how to put all the power back into your hands and make these filters work for you.

Although other applicants may know that some of these filters are in place, until now, there has been no game plan on HOW to turn the tables and make them work for YOU.

In this chapter, you'll discover how to make yourself visible to your key decision-makers—and then turn the whole thing on autopilot to make your dream opportunities come to you.

The first visibility hack—which is the focus of this chapter—is what I call N'SIDER SETTINGS. I have four N'sider Settings that will help you take back control of the job search process and get instantly noticed by recruiters and hiring managers.

My four N'sider Settings will also allow you to become a MAGNETIC Candidate. This is HUGE because instead of constantly reaching out to your dream companies, they are going to start reaching out to YOU.

(A quick heads up: the second visibility hack will be the focus of the next chapter. It's what I call the TARGETED VISIBILITY HACK, and it ensures your application NEVER gets rejected by the biggest company gatekeeper again. But more on that in chapter 5.)

PLAY TO WIN AND YOU WILL WIN

Remember, this book is all about clarity and getting a clear vision of what your DREAM JOB is, and also knowing EXACTLY what it takes to land it in DAYS, not months.

It's about removing the guesswork, cutting out wasted time, and accelerating your success with me as your mentor guiding you every step of the way.

Keep in mind that you will only succeed with my 5-step Obvious Candidate framework if you read each chapter and complete all the exercises in the CAREER COMMANDER ASSIGNMENTS. These assignments are built to be immediately infused in your job search process for RESULTS.

THE VISIBILITY HACKS THAT WILL ATTRACT RECRUITERS AND HIRING MANAGERS TO YOU LIKE A MAGNET

As I've mentioned, I'm on a mission to free 1 million job seekers from the traditional guidance that's putting them into an endless crazy cycle and to help them permanently take command over their careers. A big part of my mission comes directly from my goal to provide high-cost, corporate-sponsored tools to job seekers like you—WITHOUT the unnecessary barriers.

Here are the reasons why these Visibility Hacks are so important.

#1: These are the same Visibility Hacks that COMPANIES use to quickly and easily source their top list of candidates—which requires very little effort on their end and saves them time and money.

#2: Before I came along and merged these Visibility Hacks into my system, they were only available to executive-level job seekers through exclusive, corporate-sponsored programs.

#3: The two hacks that you'll be learning over the next two Chapters are directly responsible for shortening the job search process down to just DAYS, not Months—without sacrificing any opportunities or pay. In fact, they boost them!

VISIBILITY HACK #1: GETTING IN FRONT OF PEOPLE WHO NEED YOU 24/7

I've mentioned this in a previous chapter, but I'm going to mention it again here because it's so important: Recruiters don't magically find you out of thin air. In fact, they don't even spend much time at all searching for the right candidates. Instead, most of them use the $10,000+ a year filtering tool that's essentially "Google for the Talent Search"—**LinkedIn Recruiter**.

To find the top candidates, all a recruiter needs to do is customize several of the search filters within that tool. This presents two problems for the candidate.

One problem is that very few candidates know how to optimize their LinkedIn Profile to show up on the first page of search results for a recruiter using LinkedIn Recruiter. In fact, for any given search, there are only a select few candidates who meet all the criteria.

Another problem is that, until now, a candidate had to personally know a recruiter and all of their insider tips and secrets to appear in their search results.

With LinkedIn Recruiter, most candidates appear in a recruiter's search results just because of blind luck. Usually they happen to get lucky because their Profile aligns with or matches the recruiter's filters. That kind of luck won't last.

Also, it won't produce consistent results for different searches made by various key decision-makers.

However, there is a way to "beat" LinkedIn Recruiter—and it involves having a master-planned LinkedIn Profile specifically tailored to meet each filter.

BEATING LINKEDIN RECRUITER

The good news is that there's a way to show up as one of those top candidates EVERY SINGLE TIME.

I've created a step-by-step playbook for you to do this yourself. The only prerequisite is that you'll need to have a LinkedIn Profile Page, which you can get for free. In the coming sections of this chapter, I'll show you how to optimize your Profile in a way that gets recruiters and hiring managers flocking to YOU.

Before that, though, let's first ensure that your LinkedIn Profile Page is primed to stand out and capture attention. You're about to be getting A LOT more traffic to your Profile, and I've got great news—you've already done all the hard work!

CREATING YOUR LINKEDIN PROFILE LANDING PAGE

Are you ready to hear the make-or-break question asked by EVERY one of your audiences once they view your LinkedIn Profile? Well, it turns out it's the same question we ask ourselves every time a product catches our eye: "Why should I be interested?"

Much like your decision to either buy that product or find something better, it's those few brief moments of curiosity that can either put you in first place or cause you to be skipped over for another candidate.

The four N'sider Settings that we'll uncover later in this chapter are designed to get you TRAFFIC and VIEWS. These are the two difference-makers that will have companies coming to you so fast, you may actually have to start turning them away!

However, if you don't capture their interest the second they view your LinkedIn Profile Page, the N'sider Settings will NEVER work the way in which they're designed. That's why it's crucial that your LinkedIn Profile Page is set up to sell you as the Obvious Candidate from the very start.

Remember this, your LinkedIn Profile Page will serve as your job search's ultimate sales landing page. Yes, getting views and traffic to your Profile Page is extremely important—but if you don't have an effective way to then SELL yourself, you will never capitalize on your newfound visibility.

Here's the great news. You've already set yourself up perfectly to do this by completing the Career Commander Assignment in Chapter 3, which involved creating your Summary

Statement. (If you haven't yet completed the assignment, please go back and do it before moving any further!)

As mentioned before, the purpose of your Summary Statement isn't JUST to capture attention on your resume. It's also the foundation to be used for your Headline and About Section on LinkedIn.

So before we start opening up your Profile Page to unlimited traffic and views, let's first ensure it showcases an Attention-Grabbing Headline and an About Section that contains the 4 Story Elements needed to HOOK and stay remembered by your key decision-makers.

WRITING YOUR ATTENTION-GRABBING HEADLINE

Here's a little secret: When your audiences conduct a search in LinkedIn Recruiter, every top candidate has one common denominator—they all show the same Job Title in their Headline.

LinkedIn Recruiter's algorithm prioritizes the words in your Headline over every other section of your profile. And, as a result, it's the first thing recruiters and hiring managers see emphasized in BOLD in their search results.

So, to put it simply, your Headline is not a place on your profile where you need to reinvent the wheel. Just as a shoe store most likely has the word "Shoes" in its title, you too should begin by adding the exact DESIRED Job Title into your Headline.

This relates back to the TARGETED APPROACH in Chapter 2's "Becoming The Obvious Candidate" Exercise. To review, this is where you can simply include your current or most relevant prior title, and then add a word like "Aspiring" or "Future" in front of the TITLE of your Dream Job if you haven't yet held the position.

To illustrate your Attention-Grabbing Headline and the following steps, I want to share certain sections of a LinkedIn Profile from one of our Job Seekers University Alumni—whose identity I changed to "Noah Jobs" for this example.

Noah wanted to apply for Accounting positions when he came to us for help but was currently a Business Development Representative. So, how was he able to put "Accountant" in his Headline without "lying?" He simply added the words "Aspiring" next to his desired Job Title with absolutely ZERO penalties.

You see, LinkedIn's algorithm doesn't care about qualifying words such as "Aspiring" or "Future." Instead, the Job Title itself is the only thing it craves. So, when going for a new position, use two Job Titles in your Headline—the one that currently describes you, and the one that showcases your desired position.

Then, if you want to take your Headline even one step further, and you know the exact industry in which you would like to work and have a crucial skill you'd like to showcase, you can include them as additional keywords in your Headline. In Noah's case, it was:

"Aspiring Accountant in the Energy Section with a Focus on ERP."

Whichever method you decide to use, just remember that the most important rule is to make sure your desired Job Title is included in your Headline. It's the first step in getting the initial "View" and will show up in BOLD right next to your name when your audiences perform searches via LinkedIn Recruiter.

Also, did you notice the acronym ERP in Noah's Headline? ERP stands for enterprise resource planning, which is something that not everyone knows about. However, Noah made the right decision to include ERP in his Headline because he's sure that the key-decision makers perusing his LinkedIn definitely know what it means.

THE 4 STORY ELEMENTS OF YOUR "ABOUT" SECTION:

Once you've created your Attention-Grabbing Headline, something that you most likely already completed in Chapter 2, your key decision-makers will immediately turn their focus to your Profile Page's "About" Section. You've piqued their curiosity with your targeted headline, and now, it's time to validate that curiosity with PROOF.

Being the most critical part of your LinkedIn Profile itself, your About Section is the main copy your key decision-makers will read once they visit your Page. Think of this part of the Hook as "the quick win"—the thing you say right at the very beginning that amplifies curiosity, immediately proves it to be true, and then ends with a call to action.

Now, you might be asking yourself HOW do I actually write this in a way that includes all of that information? The answer is quite simple. We're going to go back to the oldest form of engaging communication—STORYTELLING—to break down your About Section into the 4 Story Elements and talk about how to write each one.

STORY ELEMENT 1: WHO YOU ARE

There's no better way to amplify curiosity than by telling recruiters and hiring managers you're their Obvious Candidate—and that's EXACTLY what this first Story Element will do.

Much like you started the Summary Statement of your Resume, the About Section of your LinkedIn should instantly tell your audiences Who You Are and What You Do. The only difference is that this time, you can personalize it with pronouns, like "I."

So, to begin this narrative arc and take your audiences down the path of your Story, there's a writing structure you can use to instantly draw them in. I've included an example below that our job seekers use to bring their stories to life and stand out.

As a [Desired Job Title] with a passion for [What You Do], I'm excited/thrilled to take my [Number of Years] of expertise/knowledge in [Specific Knowledge] to help the right company/organization thrive/succeed in the future.

Just to be clear, above I've written "excited/thrilled," "expertise/knowledge," "company/organization," and "thrive/succeed." In your sentence, don't copy those words verbatim. Instead, be sure to pick the most suitable word from each word pair.

Now let's look at Noah's example from his LinkedIn Profile Page.

As a Business Development Rep and Aspiring Accountant with a passion for leading complex ERP projects, I'm excited to take my 5+ years of expertise in project management and forecasting to help the right organization thrive in the future.

As you can see, Noah heightened the curiosity level of the reader without giving away the whole farm. That's something we're going to do in this second Story Element—validating curiosity through what you've accomplished.

STORY ELEMENT 2: VALIDATING CURIOSITY THROUGH ACCOMPLISHMENTS

It's one thing to tell your audiences you're precisely who they're looking for, it's another to then PROVE that to be true.

No recruiter or hiring manager will choose you just because of who you SAY you are. They also need to know you can DO the job. This is what you've set them up to CRAVE—and now it's time to prove it to be true.

To achieve this, provide them with your top 3 most impactful, relevant accomplishments that qualify you for the job. These accomplishments can be found in the Professional Experience section of your Resume and can also be reused when you get to the same section in your LinkedIn Profile.

Just make sure to write them in the same way you did before, but this time use dashes or asterisks instead of bullet points—as LinkedIn doesn't natively support bullet points.

* *[Relevant Accomplishment from Professional Experience]*

* *[Relevant Accomplishment from Professional Experience]*

* *[Relevant Accomplishment from Professional Experience]*

Returning to Noah's example, here's how he provided relevant accomplishments even though he hadn't yet worked as an Accountant:

* Created a cost accounting system as an intern with a local start-up, allowing the company to balance its books for the first time.

* Helped manage the Debate Team's budget through careful forecasting and controls, leading to three straight years of surpluses.

* Provided pro bono investment advice to the Boys & Girls Club, helping generate a 10% return.

As you can see, by referencing experiences from across his entire professional and academic history, Noah found 3 instances that would qualify him for an Accounting position.

So, just like Noah, think about your dream position, and identify three instances in your Professional history that would qualify you for the job.

STORY ELEMENT 3: YOUR TOP TRANSFERABLE SKILLS & CERTIFICATIONS

This story element is short and sweet, but it's extremely important to include for 2 reasons: #1 Your hard and soft skills move you up the search rankings in the Recruiter tool, and #2 Your hard and soft skills serve as a reference to how quickly you can be onboarded at your new company.

For now, below your 3 accomplishment statements just include a Specialties line that presents the top Skills and Certifications in your current resume. If you're having trouble coming up with 10, job descriptions from your past or similar roles can provide great context of what to include.

Specialties: [Transferable Skill #1, Transferable Skill #2, Transferable Skill #3, Transferable Skill #4, Transferable Skill #5, Transferable Skill #6, Transferable Skill #7, Transferable Skill #8, Transferable Skill #9, Transferable Skill #10]

For example, on Noah's LinkedIn Profile, he added the following line:

Specialties: Accounting, Auditing, Budgeting, Cash Flow Analysis, ERP, Forecasting, and Tax Optimization.

STORY ELEMENT 4: THE CALL TO ACTION

Once you've brought over your Skills and Certifications, you're ready for your Call to Action. The Call to Action is the statement that you're going to use at the end of your About Section that reiterates WHY you're the Obvious Candidate and gives your audiences a way to contact you.

Here's the structure of your Call to Action:

Looking for a(n) experienced/dedicated [Desired Job Title] in the [Target Location] area? Contact me at [Your Professional Email Address].

For example, on Noah's LinkedIn Profile, his Call to Action was:

Looking for a dedicated Accountant in the Seattle area? Contact me at noah.jobs@gmail.com

This easy-to-follow story path will set you up for ultimate success when floods of traffic and views start hitting your Profile Page. So, now that you've built the right foundation, are you ready to learn the secret settings that will have recruiters and hiring managers attracted to you like a magnet? Let's uncover how to turn LinkedIn Recruiter into your UNFAIR ADVANTAGE!

CAREER COMMANDER ASSIGNMENT: THE 4 N'SIDER SETTINGS TO HACK LINKEDIN RECRUITER

In this section, I'll walk you through the 4 N'sider Settings you need to hack LinkedIn Recruiter and search engine optimize yourself.

N'SIDER SETTING 1: SHOW YOU'RE OPEN TO WORK

The first N'sider Setting is: **Showing That You're Open to Work**.

When it comes to the search results in LinkedIn Recruiter, you'll have already placed yourself ahead of other candidates by infusing your Obvious Candidate Statement into your headline. BUT, you're still missing a big piece of the puzzle, which relates to showing them whether or not you're ACTUALLY looking for a job.

Recruiters and hiring managers are busy and don't want to waste valuable time reaching out to candidates who aren't searching for a new opportunity. That's why the "Open to Work" filter is one of the first boxes they check in the LinkedIn Recruiter tool.

And here's the best part: To ensure you show up at the top of their list, it's essential that your "Open to Work" setting is "on." Here's how you do that:

- Go to your LinkedIn Profile.

- Just below your number of connections, select the "I am" or "Open to" button.

- Click "Looking for a Job."

- Fill in your Job Preferences and remember to include ALL desired Titles and Locations.

Once you've done that, you'll see a section at the bottom that lets you choose who can see your "Open to Work" status—either ALL LinkedIn members or just recruiters.

If you pick ALL, then LinkedIn will add an "Open to Work" frame around your profile picture, which can be helpful.

But if you're currently in another job and are quietly searching for better opportunities, the "Recruiters Only" option is the better choice. If you pick "Recruiter Only," when people use LinkedIn Recruiter, you'll still show up in the "Open to Work" filter, yet LinkedIn will take extra measures to prevent recruiters in your current company from seeing your signal—allowing you to bulletproof yourself and have the best of both worlds.

N'SIDER SETTING 2: IMPORT YOUR CONTACTS TO GAIN COMPANY CONNECTIONS

The second N'sider Setting is: **Importing Your Contacts to Gain Company Connections.**

In LinkedIn, there are three types of "Connections," each of which refer to a different level of connection or relationship you have with another LinkedIn member:

- **1st-Degree Connections:** People with whom you are directly connected on LinkedIn because you have accepted their invitation to connect or vice versa.

- **2nd-Degree Connections:** People who are connected to your 1st-degree connections but are not directly connected to you.

- **3rd-Degree Connections:** People who are connected to your 2nd-degree connections but are not connected to you directly or through a shared connection.

Key decision-makers using LinkedIn Recruiter regularly filter their search results based on whether candidates like you have or don't have "Company Connections."

So, you may ask, "How could I possibly have a connection at every one of my known and unknown dream opportunities?" Well, while it may seem like an insurmountable task, you'd be surprised just how far your 1st, 2nd, and 3rd-degree connections can reach when you focus on building your network.

In fact, if you have just 500 1st-degree connections, your 3rd-degree network can be as large as 125 MILLION people. And yes, 3rd-degree connections count as "Company Connections" in the LinkedIn Recruiter tool.

So, taking this crazy statistic into account, how can you go about growing your network to 500 connections if you don't have them yet?

Well, you could take the traditional approach and focus on building one connection at a time. Alternatively, you could go for hundreds—or even thousands—of connections in one swoop by importing your address books into LinkedIn.

Here's the secret: Every time you email someone or create a new contact in your phone, that person gets added to the address books associated with your email accounts and smartphone, which you can easily add to LinkedIn using its Contact Import Feature.

To do this on your laptop:

- At the top of your LinkedIn home screen, click the "My Network Tab."

- Expand the "Manage My Network" section.

- Click "Contacts."

- Add all relevant email addresses to import your contacts.

- After importing your contacts, go through the list and send invitation requests to everyone you know.

To do this in your LinkedIn app on your smartphone:

- Open the LinkedIn app on your phone.

- Select "My Network" in the bottom navigation bar.

- Tap the "Contacts" icon.

- Choose the "Add Contacts" feature.

- After importing your contacts, go through the list and send invitation requests to everyone you know.

By doing these steps, you will open yourself up to MILLIONS of opportunities, AND you're also giving yourself a great chance to pass one of the STRICTEST filters your audiences use.

N'SIDER SETTING 3: FOLLOW YOUR TARGET COMPANIES

The third N'sider Setting is: **Following Your Target Companies**.

After getting "In" with your key decision-makers through WHO you know, there's one last filter you can control, and it can be done by following your target companies.

While most of these N'sider Settings involve being proactive and taking the lead, this is one time you want to be a follower.

And to show your key decision-makers that you're qualified AND interested, always hit the "Follow" button for any organization that you're even slightly interested in.

It may seem like a tiny commitment, but it's an incredibly easy way to place yourself in the "Engaged with Talent Brand" filter in LinkedIn Recruiter.

LinkedIn lets you follow up to 1,000 organizations. I recommend following all the companies who have postings for your dream jobs.

N'SIDER SETTING 4: SEARCH ENGINE OPTIMIZE YOURSELF

The fourth N'sider Setting is: **Search Engine Optimizing Yourself.**

The previous N'sider Settings related to optimizing your LinkedIn Profile. This one is about optimizing yourself and your LinkedIn Profile to Google so that your LinkedIn shows up in Google search results when your name is searched.

To show up on both LinkedIn AND Google—which are the two major search engines used by your key decision-makers—do the following steps.

First, make your LinkedIn Profile public so that Google can find you:

- Go to your LinkedIn Profile.

- Click "Edit Public Profile & URL"

- Turn your Profile's public visibility to "On."

- Make as many components of your Profile public— and findable by Google—as you're comfortable with.

Second, make your LinkedIn Profile easy to find by Google's PageRank Algorithm, which can be done by including your Name in your Profile URL. You'll do this by creating a custom URL for your LinkedIn:

- Go to the "Edit Public Profile & URL" section.

- Next to your current URL, click the pen icon.

- Change your custom URL to include your name. I suggest using the following format: first name, middle initial, then last name. If there are many people with the same name as you, consider using the following format: first name, middle initial, last name, then job title.

SHARE YOUR LINKEDIN PROFILE PAGE URL WITH THE CAREER COMMANDERS COMMUNITY

These N'sider Settings are straightforward and simple—but if you aren't optimizing them in the right way, then the reality is that you won't show up to your key decision-makers.

So, when reading the previous sections, did you apply each of the above four N'sider Settings to your LinkedIn? If you haven't yet, be sure to do that now.

You only have to do it once to reap the rewards. And the couple of minutes it takes to set everything up and turn it on autopilot will open you up to a whole new world of opportunity.

Once you've turned on all the settings, be sure to share your new, custom LinkedIn Profile URL with the Career Commanders Community. This is a GREAT way to boost your network and connections and also showcase yourself to the decision-makers we have in our community.

And if you're an introvert like me and find it unnatural to share your Profile with others, here's a word of encouragement. Unlike Facebook or Instagram, LinkedIn is not a place where you need to share life updates to get engagement. It's a powerful tool that can connect you with your dream job in a way no other platform can.

And it's a professional network of which you need to take advantage because there's a battle going on to find you every single day—where your key decision-makers are searching to find the Obvious Candidate to fill their NEEDS.

So, share your Profile with the goal of landing your dream job. It's meant to be seen because that's how you'll get results!

CHAPTER 5: GET PAST THE GATEKEEPERS

Congratulations on reading the first four chapters so far and being someone who finishes what you start! Remember, a big part of success is just showing up. Another big part, of course, is actually doing the work.

So, even though this is the last chapter related to my 5-Step framework to become the MOST Obvious Candidate, be sure to read it and do the work. (And, yes, I have bonus chapters you can look forward to after I wrap up this final step in my framework—but let's hold off on those until we get there.)

So, in this chapter, I'm going to show you the second Visibility Hack. This will empower you to get past the gatekeepers and ensure you get seen by the key decision-makers at your dream jobs.

Today is all about giving you the shortcut you need to shorten your job search down to just DAYS and turn a process built for the COMPANY into one that will become your greatest advantage.

VISIBILITY HACK #2: HOW TO ENSURE YOUR APPLICATION DOESN'T GET REJECTED

I want to peel back the curtain on one of the most misunderstood parts of your job search—the application process. You see, there are reasons why companies aren't contacting you, aren't inviting you to an initial interview, and aren't inviting you back for second and third interviews.

But it's NOT your fault. It's because of a flawed process that, until now, has been totally out of your control.

And do you know the main culprit?

It's the Applicant Tracking System (ATS)—the automated software that companies use to filter resumes for specific keywords that match their job description.

But here's the kicker. As a job seeker, you have no real way of knowing the EXACT keywords you need to include—making it a true guessing game.

This unfair approach underscores my worrying claim that the job search process is built to benefit the COMPANY, when it should instead benefit CANDIDATES like you.

HOW TO BEAT APPLICANT TRACKING SYSTEMS AND TAKE BACK CONTROL

Earlier I mentioned that I want to provide expensive corporate tools directly to you for FREE. While that may sound too good to be true, I want to remind you that I grew up in a family business that for over 30 years has partnered with companies to help their departing employees find jobs.

Importantly, those high-cost, corporate-sponsored programs used exclusive corporate tools that weren't made available to general job seekers.

A major reason why these programs produced better results than the average job search process is because they got applicants through the Applicant Tracking Systems. They did this by reverse-engineering the most common ATS's used by companies today. And that's also what I do in my system. The difference is that in my system I'm giving them to you—regardless of whether you're an executive or not—at NO COST.

I'll do this by showing you HOW to add those missing keywords back into your resume, without doing all the manual work by yourself or creating a new resume from scratch every time.

GET PAST THE GATEKEEPERS WITH TARGETED VISIBILITY

The Visibility Hack I explore in this chapter, just like the Visibility Hack in the previous chapter, will have recruiters and hiring managers attracted to you like a magnet.

Right now, I'm about to be really blunt about something because my goal is to cut out all the nonsense, show you the TRUTH, and help you land your dream job in record time.

There is a hidden game that's being played deep underneath the surface of your job search. It's a game that the hiring company unashamedly uses to make their lives easier and cut their costs. And it's one that, regrettably, can leave you hanging out to dry if you don't know how to capitalize on it.

A REAL-LIFE EXAMPLE TO ILLUSTRATE THE GAME COMPANIES PLAY WITH YOUR RESUME

To show you what I mean, and how it's maybe already hurt you, I want to tell you the story about Alex.

For over ten years, Alex has been a high-level operations manager. He's the type of guy who does high-quality work, doesn't let anything slip through the cracks, and has a long list of professional achievements.

In other words, hiring Alex should be a no-brainer. But after being laid-off due to a leadership change at his job, he simply couldn't secure a new job. His networking connections weren't working out, and for some reason, he was hardly getting ANY interviews.

Alex couldn't figure out what was wrong. From his perspective, he was doing everything right in his job search. Yet with each unanswered application or rejection email, he felt like a sick joke was being played on him.

He had just assumed that his resume accurately communicated his accomplishments in a way that would make him desirable to recruiters and hiring managers.

Still, no matter how many jobs he applied for, he wasn't making any progress. Deep down, he knew that SOMETHING needed to change. He just didn't know what it was. That's when he hired me to help him get out of this crazy cycle.

Quickly, I realized that Alex had one of the best-written resumes I had ever seen. It hooked his audiences, communicated his value, and showcased his expertise. On the one hand, he didn't need to change a single word in his resume. But on the other hand, he DID.

You see, Alex was only using this one resume to apply for each dream job he came across. On the surface, that makes sense, right?

But here's what it didn't do. His resume DIDN'T ever get seen by the actual key decision-makers at his top opportunities. Why? Because although his resume had GREAT words, it had the WRONG words to pass the Applicant Tracking System (ATS) at each one of his target companies.

THIS is the game companies play, and it has worked against me, it has worked against Alex, and it WILL work against you—unless you know how to BEAT them at their own game.

When I told Alex about this, he said, "That couldn't possibly be happening. I'm qualified. There's no way the ATS is filtering out my resume."

I said, "Alex, you ARE super qualified and your resume is awesome. But the reality is that to get to the people who will hire you and see those qualifications, you first need to make sure your resume passes the ATS. And to achieve that, your resume needs to have the EXACT keywords the ATS is programmed to find and identify."

Alex's eyes opened wide.

"Synonyms don't even count," I said. "You need the EXACT keywords."

This is when the switch flipped for him in how he viewed his job search. He said, "You're telling me that the reason I'm dealing with all this stress and rejection is because my resume is missing a few keywords?"

I nodded.

"Ok," Alex said. "What can I do to make sure I have them?"

That's when I showed him our Application Master Key Tool. This tool reverse-engineered the specific ATS used by his target company and showed him EXACTLY what keywords he was missing for each one of his applications, creating what I call an "ATS-Certified" version of his resume.

Unfortunately, Alex became instantly overwhelmed because he thought he was going to need to re-write his resume for each new application, which would take hours every day.

However, he wasn't seeing the whole picture. Yes, Alex would need to submit a new "ATS-Certified" version of his resume for each application to ensure he made it into the final round of candidates. BUT, it wouldn't require him creating a totally new resume each time.

All it would require is TWEAKING his BASE RESUME to ensure it has those tailored keywords to make him one of the final remaining candidates.

Did you notice my previous reference to a "base resume"? If that term is new to you, think of a base resume as a foundational document that outlines your summary statement, work experience, education, skills, and qualifications. It serves as a starting point that you can customize for different job applications by tailoring the KEYWORDS in it to match the requirements of the ATS and the position for which you're applying. You don't attach your base resume unchanged to your applications. Instead, you add or subtract certain KEYWORDS to it, ensuring that the customized resume you end up attaching to your application gets seen by your key decision-makers.

Importantly, these keyword tweaks don't have to be done manually anymore. In my ultimate job search solution—aka my "secret sauce"—that I'll reveal in the later chapters of this book, I'll reveal the expertly crafted prompts you can use to AUTOMATE the entire process, FIND the missing keywords, and ADD them into your BASE RESUME.

And this is precisely what Alex did once I showed him how the whole process worked. He found the job description of his dream job, used our Application Master Key Tool to compare the job description to his BASE RESUME, and then used our prompts to add the missing keywords into his CUSTOMIZED RESUME.

All in all, it took Alex around 10 minutes to use our Application Master Key Tool to create a customized resume for his first application—with very little manual writing on his end.

Can you imagine that? That means that Alex—and you too—could send out 5 applications for his dream jobs in UNDER an hour, all WHILE ensuring he gets past the ATS and is one of the final candidates remaining to be seen by his key decision-makers.

And that's exactly what Alex did and why he had 3 OFFERS on the table after going through his interview process. And it's also worth noting that the 3 interviews that came with those offers were lined up only 2 DAYS after Alex applied for the jobs!

IT'S TIME TO BEAT COMPANIES AT THEIR OWN GAME

This works because, not only are you beating the companies at their own game, but you're also basing it all on YOU and the work you've done to become the MOST Obvious Candidate.

Companies are always trying to automate the most time-consuming parts of their businesses, including their application process.

In fact, OVER 70% of submitted resumes are now reviewed by an Applicant Tracking System before they ever reach human eyes.

More importantly, a whopping 99% of Fortune 500 companies are currently using an ATS.

THE GAME ISN'T FAIR…BUT YOU CAN BEAT IT!

But here's the thing—the ATS is not some super-intelligent robot that should keep you up at night. Yes, it is the main reason why your application isn't getting SEEN and you aren't getting the interview. And is that unfair? ABSOLUTELY. It's a one-dimensional system that filters out countless great candidates every day.

But, the reality is that it's not going to change. And companies LOVE how much time and money it saves them in their hiring process.

Which means that instead of focusing on how negatively it affects you, you need to turn your full attention to BEATING it. And luckily, with our Application Master Key Tool, that process just got a LOT simpler.

You see, there isn't any special magic behind the Applicant Tracking System. It's not inherently discriminatory or out to get you. It's just following the specific instructions given to it by the company.

And that all comes down to the keywords in the JOB DESCRIPTION.

HOW THE ATS WORKS

When a company posts a job description for any open position they either input specific keywords for the ATS to track, or they get their ATS to suggest relevant keywords FOR them.

Think about a hospital that wants to hire a nurse. In their job description, the hospital might have keywords related to that specific nursing position, such as the following:

- Electronic health records.
- IV therapy.

- Wound care.

- Infection control.

Or think about a company that would like to hire a marketing professional. In their job description, the company might have keywords related to that specific marketing position, such as the following:

- Content creation.

- Lead generation.

- Marketing analytics.

- A/B testing.

Then, when you submit your resume, the ATS extracts data from your resume to rank and sort you based on how well the keywords in your resume match the ones it chose to filter for in the job description.

Returning to the nursing and marketing examples, the company ATS will scan all the resumes, checking if they have or don't have those exact keywords. If a resume has enough of them required to pass the ATS, then that nurse or marketer will go to the top of the pile. If a resume doesn't have enough of those exact keywords—remember, synonyms don't count—then that nurse or marketer will go to the bottom of the pile.

What you need to know is that, for candidates who DON'T make it through, the ATS is the one responsible for that automated rejection email that makes you want to grimace and shake your fists. But for the candidates who DO make it through—which is usually purely on blind luck—the ATS will then track their progress, schedule interviews, and sometimes even administer pre-employment tests.

This process—which is mostly carried out by the technology—is WHY the job search process takes an average of 5 months. It's why it's working AGAINST you, and it's why the power truly is being taken OUT of your hands.

THE SOLUTION

BUT, there is a solution. It's just that, until now, to get the solution you'd either have to pay thousands of dollars OR be in a 5-figure, corporate-sponsored program.

That's not the case anymore, though. Remember, I'm on a mission to free one million people from the chains of traditional job search methods and help them take back control of their careers. And one of the biggest parts of that mission is BREAKING DOWN BARRIERS.

And that's why, not only do you get unlimited, lifetime access to our Application Master Key Tool in the ultimate job search solution that I'm about to share later in this book, but you also get a peek behind the curtain and a FREE scan of your resume as a bonus for reading this book.

This knowledge is NOT available to the general public. Your competition doesn't know WHAT keywords to include or how to get their resume past the ATS. But you WILL.

READER BONUS

I want to offer you a free bonus—but there's a catch. This offer is ONLY for those readers—you, hopefully!—who have completed ALL of the CAREER COMMANDER assignments in the previous chapters. If that's you, great!

Here's what I'd like you to do: send me your RESUME and the URL for the job posting of your DREAM JOB.

I will then use our Application Master Key Tool to scan the two and give you a report on how much your resume matches—or doesn't match—the job opportunity, plus a list of all keywords you're missing from your resume.

Remember, the Application Master Key Tool is our industry-leading tool that reverse-engineers the most common Applicant Tracking Systems and provides you with the EXACT missing keywords that are holding your application back from making it to human eyes.

I'm giving this away for free to incentivize you to play to WIN. As I wrote previously, I can urge you to be COMMITTED to completing my 5-step framework to becoming the MOST Obvious Candidate. And I can tell you about all of the phenomenal benefits that come to JOB SEEKERS who follow my system. But you're the one who has to DECIDE to commit and then FULLY BELIEVE that you are indeed committed.

And if that's YOU, then just provide me with your RESUME and the URL for the job posting of your DREAM JOB at TheJobSeekersUniversity.com/masterkeyreport. Also, please note that I will NOT share your information with anyone else. Your resume will not be seen by anyone other than our team of experts who create your custom report.

CAREER COMMANDER ASSIGNMENT: THE MASTER KEY: UNLOCKED

So, to ensure you're taking full advantage of the Reader Bonus, let's learn HOW you can immediately put the power BACK into your hands and get yourself past the ultimate gatekeeper—the ATS.

Before I get into the step-by-step process of how to use the Application Master Key Tool, it's important to know its purpose—which is to take a complex software system, the ATS, and give you simple, actionable instructions you can follow to easily beat it.

STEP 1: ANALYZE THE JOB DESCRIPTION OF YOUR DREAM JOB

First, you need to find the job description of your Dream Opportunity. Then remember this tip: You only need to identify the actual MEAT of the job description itself—which includes the details that the ATS will consider when it scans your resume.

For instance, even if the job description mentions the company's name and its location, you can ignore those details because the ATS won't scan for them in your resume.

Here are all of the sections in the job description that you should pay particular attention to because it is these areas and their keywords that the ATS will put its laser-focus on when analyzing your resume:

- The responsibilities and requirements of your dream job.
- The purpose of your dream job.
- The qualifications centered around the role.
- Any other tasks or responsibilities associated with the role.

Take a look at the following examples for a good guideline.

Key information 1:

The purpose of the Sales Account Executive is to meet and exceed sales objectives in their assigned territory by promoting and selling outdoor advertising to qualified advertisers. An Account Executive (AE) is expected to use professional sales techniques and develop long-term advertising relationships that grow our advertising sales.

Key information 2:

What we're looking for in YOU:

- Comfort making cold calls over the phone and in-person.

- Ability to make oral presentations and clearly articulate policies and procedures.

- Align with our values of inclusivity and effectively communicate with people of various social, cultural, economic, and educational backgrounds.

- Motivation to learn new technology and systems.

- Ability to exhibit effective time management and self-organization.

- Willingness to immerse yourself in the outdoor advertising industry with the intent of selling its benefits to businesses and customers.

- Ability to communicate professionally both verbally and in writing.

- Ability to perform effectively under fluctuating workloads.

- A knack for making connections and gaining the trust of others.

- Ability to meet a sales quota and utilize general sales techniques.

- Intrinsic self-motivation to overcome challenges and meet goals.

- Resilience in response to rejection.

Education and experience:

- Current and valid driver's license required.

- College degree preferred.

- Previous outdoor advertising sales experience preferred.

- Proficiency in Microsoft Office Suite.

- CRM experience preferred.

Key information #3:

Regularly, you will:

- Meet and exceed sales targets and monitor personal sales data and reports.

- Target businesses in the assigned area and visit each established client as well as competitor's clients in a specified time frame.

- Exhibit working knowledge of local and national competition.

- Cluster accounts to work them efficiently.

- Identify potential growth areas and open new accounts.

- Use our computer tools to locate prospects and follow up on leads, as well as prepare proposals, written presentations, and research.

- Develop presentation skills by utilizing computer tools, and present to clients regularly.

- Develop new product knowledge and selling skills.

- Actively participate in sales meetings, regional meetings, seminars, and trade shows.

- Maintain daily, weekly, and monthly sales plans a month in advance.

- Follow up on all client production orders and problem-solve any issues that may arise.

- Maintain organized and up-to-date records of clients and sales activity.

STEP 2: COMPARE THE JOB DESCRIPTION AGAINST YOUR BASE RESUME

Next you will want to check if those keywords from the previously identified parts of the job description are in your base resume.

And once you've identified both your base resume and the job description you're comparing it against, it's time to use the Application Master Key Tool.

The Tool will provide to you the information you need to tweak it—or even add to it—while reducing any guesswork or writer's block.

The Application Master Key Tool will provide you with what's called a Match Rate, which goes from 0% to 100%. A low Match Rate means that your resume doesn't match many keywords, and it will likely be blocked by the ATS and will never be seen by a human. A high Match Rate means your resume matches numerous keywords, and it will likely pass the company's ATS. For instance, if your Match Rate is 75% or above, then your resume is what we call "ATS-Certified," ensuring that your resume makes it into the final round of candidates and gets SEEN by your key decision-makers.

Remember that the Tool reverse-engineers the specific ATS used by your target company and searches for EXACT keywords. And if you are missing those keywords from your resume, they are holding you back. But you can flip this to your advantage. Indeed, knowing and acting on this can give you an UNFAIR ADVANTAGE over other candidates. Why? Because your competition won't know anything about this, and you'll be able to make a copy of your base resume, add the previously missing keywords to it, and use that customized resume to apply for that specific position.

THE APPLICATION MASTER KEY TOOL

Now let me address a common question really quickly. What happens if you get your customized report from the Application Master Key Tool, add in as many keywords as you can, and still don't hear back? Well, it doesn't mean that this won't work or that I'm misleading you. This is a process, and you need to let it play out.

Think about it this way. Maybe your target company is in the minority and doesn't yet have an ATS. Or, maybe the company is really only accepting applications from internal candidates, yet didn't mention that on the job description. Maybe you unknowingly applied for a position that's already been filled. Or maybe, the job posting was old and the company didn't take it down.

These things happen. And that's why later in this book, I'm going to show you how to get unlimited access to this tool AND the cheat codes that automate the keyword revisions process FOR you.

THE APPLICATION MASTER KEY TOOL + THE CHEAT CODES = THE ULTIMATE SHORTCUT TO YOUR DREAM JOB

The magic of this tool REALLY comes to life when it's used alongside our Cheat Codes to 10X your application output. I would be doing you a disservice if I said, "Hey just use this tool once, and you'll land the job."

Can that happen? Absolutely! And there have been many job seekers who have landed their dream jobs that way.

10X'ING YOUR APPLICATION OUTPUT IS THE KEY

But, the real value in this comes from what it can do for you on a macro-level. You usually don't marry the first person you date, right? But if you know the type of person you want to marry, and know EXACTLY where to find them and how to communicate with them, the chances are great you'll find your soulmate. And you'll find them a lot quicker than someone who doesn't know where to look or know what they want.

Well, sorry to bring up any past dating memories, but this same concept exists in your job search. Not every company will be the best fit, BUT there will be ones that are—and they will outnumber the ones that aren't.

And my ultimate solution that I'll share later on in this book has been purposefully built for you to put this process as a whole to work for yourself. You'll use the Application Master Key Tool to quickly scan your resume against the job description of your dream job. You'll use the Cheat Codes to automate the process of adding all the missing keywords you truthfully and realistically can. And then, you will use the Master Application Key Tool again to re-scan your resume and get it as close as possible to a 75% Match Score, or preferably even higher.

It will take you around 10 minutes to create an "ATS-Certified" resume to attach to your application, instead of it taking days or months to figure out why you're never hearing back.

Even more, if you DON'T want to do it yourself, just schedule a quick call with us at TheJobSeekersUniversity.com. My team of Job Search Architects and I will create your "ATS-Certified'" Resumes FOR you as a part of our Done-for-You Job Search service!

When you add this targeted volume with a resume that WILL pass the ATS the result is SUCCESS! And it will come in the form of interviews, and then taking your pick between the multiple great job offers that are on the table!

CAREER COMMANDER ASSIGNMENT

Now, it's time for the final exercises in my 5-Step framework to make you the MOST Obvious Candidate. Completing these assignments will get you seen, catapult you ahead of your competitors, and potentially even get you HIRED at your top dream opportunity right now.

As always, you're encouraged to share your results in our Career Commanders Community. Just visit CareerCommanders.com and join our Facebook and LinkedIn groups.

First, identify the resume you're going to use to get your scan with the Application Master Key Tool. Save it as your first and last name, then include the word "resume" at the end, such as "John Smith resume.docx."

Second, find an online posting of your highest-priority dream job. Then collect the following information about the job:

- Job title.

- Company name.

- The URL to the job posting.

Lastly, I encourage you to add your name and dream job to the following commitment statement:

I, [NAME], a future [YOUR DREAM JOB], have successfully completed the 5-Step framework for becoming the MOST Obvious Candidate! I have discovered the New Way of Job Searching and know exactly what it takes to land my dream job in DAYS, not months.

I can and will beat the outside forces actively working against me in my job search process, and I have clarity on the exact action plan I need to take going forward to shine a spotlight on myself that companies can't miss. My job search is not a game of luck. It's a game of strategy and choosing the right system!

Like previous assignments, you could type out the above statement—with your name and dream job in the appropriate spots, of course—and then print and sign the statement.

Or you could record a video of yourself saying the above statement into the camera.

And if you're a member of our Career Commanders Community, be sure to share in the community the outcomes of each of the above exercises.

THANK YOU!

In the past five chapters, it has been an HONOR to write about my 5-Step Framework for helping you become the MOST Obvious Candidate. But don't stop reading now. I've got three bonus chapters for you!

In the next chapter, I'll show you how to STAND OUT against other applicants in the final stages of your job search.

In chapter 7, I'll explore how you can add thousands of dollars to your final salary WITHOUT risking your offer.

And last but not least, in chapter 8, I've got a big surprise for you!

CHAPTER 6: THE ONE: HOW TO STAND OUT AGAINST YOUR COMPETITION AND WIN THE FINAL STAGES OF YOUR JOB SEARCH

Congratulations! By understanding HOW to ensure you pass the Applicant Tracking System, you have just solidified your place as a very TOP applicant at your dream opportunities.

Separating yourself from the average 75%-95% of candidates who don't pass the ATS is certainly a monumental feat. But you're not reading this to be in a small minority. You're reading this to be what I like to call "The One"—the person who GETS the job.

The reality is that only one candidate lands the job. In this chapter, we'll explore what it takes in the final stages of your job search to go from "A Final Candidate" to "The Final Candidate."

Here's a warning, though. To become "The One," you need to take the road less traveled. To distinguish yourself from the competition, you need to be willing to do the things that others won't do.

And I have great news—the final stages of your job search are actually the EASIEST to win. Why? Because most job seekers in the market are plagued with false beliefs and are stressed out of their minds—causing most of your competition to shy away or make mistakes, and ultimately lose the job.

WINNING this phase of your job search comes down to two very important phases: **Networking and Interviewing.**

What was your reaction right now as you read those two words? Stress? Anxiety? Thoughts of putting this book down and shoving it into a drawer?

HOLD ON! Networking and Interviewing have derailed millions of job seekers from finding the success right around the corner that awaits them, and that's because they believe the LIES told them by traditional job advice.

By the end of this chapter, you'll see just how easy Networking and Interviewing the New Way can really be. In fact, I want to challenge you right now to FORGET everything you've been told about or have experienced with these two subjects. With Networking, forget the awkwardness and stress that comes with it. With Interviewing, forget the hours of trying to memorize thousands of different answers to questions you could be asked in the interview.

Are you ready to become "The One?" If so, join me in this chapter and get ready to reap the same rewards experienced by thousands of others who have learned how to Network and Interview the RIGHT way!

NETWORK THE NEW WAY

"Networking is the favorite part of my job search process"—said no one ever, right?

If you're anything like I was, you probably think Networking is a game of who you know. That has some truth to it, but it doesn't change the fact that Networking is inherently unnatural.

You could be the most confident extrovert in the room. You could have a larger social circle than a young European billionaire. But that still doesn't change the fact that no one really WANTS to go out of their way to ask someone else for a favor. It's stressful to put yourself in a vulnerable position and risk rejection or awkwardness.

But here's the reality: Despite Networking being inherently unnatural, Networking with the goal of getting a REFERRAL is one of the biggest advantages you can have in your ENTIRE job search.

Why? Consider these statistics. While Referred Candidates often make up only a mere 7% of all applicants, they account for a whopping 40% of all hires.[1]

Yet this leads to a dilemma: While a Referral is THE difference-maker in going from random OUTSIDER to instant INSIDER, the stress and anxiety associated with Networking prevent most job seekers from ever getting started.

That's why in this book, I want to give you a plan to ditch the Old Way of Networking—and all the false beliefs that come with it. In the New Way of Networking, you'll see that all the sketchiness and awkwardness can be removed from Networking, ultimately empowering you to get a Referral at ANY organization, regardless of who you know.

And guess what? You can do the ENTIRE thing from behind the comfort of your own computer screen!

---

1. Stephanie Sparks, "4 Reasons to Invest in Employee Referrals," February 2024, Jobvite, https://www.jobvite.com/blog/4-reasons-to-invest-in-employee-referrals/

You see, Networking comes down to two objectives: **Finding Commonality and Creating Commonality.**

And if you decide to take the Traditional Approach to Networking, finding and creating commonality WILL come down to knowing the "right" people, getting lucky, and being a fearless extrovert who commands the room.

Luckily, you can leave the Traditional Way in the past—right where it belongs. Because there IS a better way, and it taps into the power of LinkedIn to break down the barriers of Networking.

Instead of knowing just the "right people," everyone you know is the "right person." Instead of getting lucky, you make your own luck. And instead of being a fearless extrovert, ANYONE can network—even from behind the comfort of their own computer screen.

Networking doesn't have to be thought of as an exclusive club that revolves around status and age-old relationships. Think of it as a modern game that requires modern solutions. To help you adopt this mindset, I want to share Gabby's story.

HOW GABBY UNLOCKED THE HIDDEN POTENTIAL OF LINKEDIN

When Gabby hired me to help her with her job search, she was at a loss. Coming from an HR background and being a naturally extroverted person, she had MANY of connections.

So she always assumed that if anything unexpected happened in her career, she could rely on her network to find new opportunities quickly.

Here's the thing. After working in corporate HR for over 7 years, Gabby was unexpectedly let go as a result of economic factors out of her control. Thinking she could rely on her network to find even better opportunities, she put her full effort into a LinkedIn Networking strategy that consisted of liking and sharing posts of peers, and even posting personal marketing statements that outlined why she was looking for a job and what strengths she would bring to a company.

There was a problem, though. Gabby wasn't receiving ANY interest. Days passed, weeks passed, and eventually, 4 months had passed before she decided a change needed to be made.

And when she invested in our **20 Day Job Search Program**, she finally understood WHY her current strategy was failing. On the surface, it looked as if she was doing all the right things. She had tons of connections. She was active on LinkedIn. And she was communicating that she was open to work.

But, she wasn't taking the ACTUAL steps to find and create COMMONALITY with those who could realistically help out at her top opportunities. Once she learned how to identify the EXACT professionals who could turn into Ideal Referrals at her target companies, and then create commonality with them in a natural and non-threatening way, her opportunities TOOK OFF!

She went from spending hours on LinkedIn every day, to finding Ideal Referrals and communicating with them in just minutes. Even better, she didn't need to ever meet with them face-to-face. She did it all via her computer!

Gabby had people ready to go to bat for her within days of changing her strategy, and it actually led to several companies reaching out to her to see if she would be interested in their opportunity. Talk about putting the power back in her hands! Just hear it from her.

Gabby: "Life before Tommy's Networking secrets? Let's just say, I was the queen of likes and shares, thinking that's all it took to get noticed for my next big career move. Spoiler alert: It wasn't.

But after diving into Tommy's system, my whole LinkedIn strategy flipped. I learned that there's way more to the platform than just socializing and collecting connections. Tommy showed me the hidden playground underneath the surface of LinkedIn —like, how to get noticed by recruiters with just a few tweaks and how to network to find my Ideal Referrals.

I stopped playing the posting game and started a targeted strategy that got me popping up on all the right radars. And guess what? Companies started reaching out to me! I felt like the hot commodity for once! And just two weeks after I implemented

Tommy's strategies, one of my dream companies came to me with an offer I couldn't refuse!

Thanks to Tommy, I went from just another LinkedIn user to the one they're all looking to hire. If you're ready to make yourself a magnet, you need to check out Tommy's system!"

So if you want to go from an old Networking strategy that depends on who you know, to one where ANYONE ANYWHERE can turn into your Ideal Referral, here's what you need to know.

The New Way of Networking all centers around finding and creating COMMONALITY. Now, when I refer to commonality, I'm referring to people who both WANT to help you and CAN help you. These kinds of people are otherwise known as your IDEAL REFERRAL.

THE GOLDEN LINK: FINDING YOUR IDEAL REFERRAL

Traditional approaches to Networking make finding your Ideal Referral extremely challenging. But it doesn't have to be that way. In fact, anyone who's still living in that reality is missing out on the real magic of Networking, and as a result, forgoing a multitude of opportunities.

So, what IS the magic behind finding your Ideal Referral? It's knowing the RIGHT way to use the online directory that allows you to get a referral from ANYONE—LinkedIn.

When it comes to finding your best options, LinkedIn will do all the work for you. You just need to know how to direct it to the RIGHT types of people.

In our system, you'll learn how to become an Instant Insider at ANY of your top opportunities, whether you currently know anyone in the organization or not.

BUT WHAT IF ...

Here's an all-too-common reality faced by many networkers: "But what if you've exhausted all your options and still can't find an Ideal Referral?"

Maybe you want to work at a small business, and they just don't have a large enough LinkedIn presence to utilize. Or maybe you're still growing your connections on LinkedIn and your Network isn't yet big enough to work for you.

Whatever your case, I WILL NOT leave you hanging out to dry. There's one fail-safe way to CREATE Commonality and get your Ideal Referral. You see, there's a secret feature on LinkedIn that's hidden SO well, it's actually in plain sight. But very few people use it for its intended purpose—to get a referral from ANYONE.

PROFESSIONAL "WINKS"

LinkedIn Profile Views are the professional "winks" that can open the door for conversation with ANY employee at your target company.

A Profile View alert on LinkedIn is a notification that informs you when someone has viewed your LinkedIn Profile. This feature lets you know who has shown interest in your profile, allowing you to gauge your visibility and reach on the platform. But know this: Profile View alerts go "both" ways. That is, whenever you click on and scroll through someone else's LinkedIn Profile, they receive an alert about YOU.

Millions of LinkedIn users notice the profile view alerts that pop up in their emails or on-screen notifications—but, most of them miss the point of WHY LinkedIn is showing them.

Remember, at its core LinkedIn is NOT just another social network. And to treat Profile Views as a sort of popularity contest misses the purpose for which they were designed.

So, why does LinkedIn take the extra effort to send you Profile View alerts? Because it's a social platform centered on GROWING your Professional Network.

And there's no better way to CREATE Commonality than with people who are already interested in YOU—the ultimate Networking accelerator. Better yet, you can use Profile Views to go on OFFENSE—giving your potential Referrals a "wink" without EVER having to put yourself in an awkward situation.

The only thing stopping you is the lack of a proven system—which we're here to change. As a matter of fact, the process of giving and receiving a professional "wink" really comes down to just a few steps.

STEP 1: VISIBILITY

So let's start with the first step: **Making Sure Your Profile is Visible.**

If your goal is to get a prospect to view YOUR profile, you can incentivize them to do so by first "winking" at them and showing up in THEIR notifications. However, all your work will be for nothing if you don't have the right Visibility Settings turned on.

To make sure that you have the appropriate LinkedIn Visibility Settings:

- At the top of your LinkedIn page, click the "Me" icon.
- Select "Settings & Privacy."
- On the left side of the page, click "Visibility."
- Click "Profile Viewing Options."
- Then select "Your Name and Headline."

Doing this will ensure that when you visit another person's profile, they'll get a notification that includes both your name and your headline.

I recommend not leaving this in "Private Mode" because that would prevent prospects from seeing your name and what you do.

You'll also never get notified when someone, including prospects, views your profile. So, to gain access to both, be sure you're as visible as possible.

STEP 2: PLANTING

The second step is: Planting Your Seeds.

Do this by:

- Going to your target company's LinkedIn Page. On that page, you'll see all the employees of that company who are on LinkedIn.

- Select your geographic location. This will change the search results so they only show employees at your location.

- Find the "Filters Feature" text box. In this box, it will have the words "Search employees by title, keyword, or school." In that box, type in the name of your Desired Position. The search results will change to only show you employees of that company who have that job title.

The people who are now shown on your screen can be thought of as members of your future work team. They are the BEST people to whom you should begin giving professional "winks."

Now, I recommend fighting the temptation to message everyone in those filtered search results. Instead, click on each profile and scroll through each profile.

Since you've made yourself visible, your activity will show up in each Prospect's notifications as "[Your Name, Headline] viewed your Profile"—setting you up PERFECTLY for a "wink" back.

And while you may be wondering if this is a bit too invasive, I promise you it's not. Think of it this way: LinkedIn wouldn't send a notification if it didn't want to promote this occurrence.

Remember, LinkedIn's main goal is to help you build your Professional Network, and profile views are a vital part of its relationship economy. So, don't be afraid to use LinkedIn the way it's MEANT to be used.

STEP 3: GROW THEN HARVEST

After planting your seeds, the next step is **Letting Them Grow—and then Harvesting Them.**

This can be the hardest part of the process because it requires WAITING to reap the fruits of your labor.

Keep this in mind: The people who are most active on LinkedIn are job seekers, recruiters, and business owners. Because of this, the person whose Profile you viewed may not go on LinkedIn every week.

But here's the great news: LinkedIn sends weekly emails alerting your Prospects of their Profile Views. Which means that even if they're not regularly active on LinkedIn, you'll still make your way STRAIGHT to their inbox.

And the best part is that you'll get notified the same way when they "wink" back. Just keep an eye on your email, or visit LinkedIn daily and look at your notifications bell—as there will be a red "Alert" icon when you have a new view.

STEP 4: CONNECT

When interest IS reciprocated, you'll be ready for the final part of the process: **Sending a Personalized Connection Request,** and once they accept, a LinkedIn Message.

Of course, we've got you covered with every Networking Campaign script you'll need in your job search in our Messaging Manual—the done-for-you response guide found in our **20 Day Job Search Program** that eliminates all awkwardness and saves you precious time in your Networking Process.

So, as you're going through the process of Profile Viewing, remember this: There is NO substitute for a thorough profile review when you find a prospect worthy of a connection.

Why? Because their Profile might contain all sorts of additional information you can use when Networking with them. So, keep your ultimate goal of an Ideal Referral in mind, and capitalize on the little-used but HIGHLY effective strategy of Profile Views in your journey to find those who both WANT TO help you and CAN help you.

It's crucial to leave NO stone left unturned when it comes to your Network. And if you are keen to learn the true roadmap to getting a referral from ANYONE—regardless of whether you know them already or not—our Networking Magic training in the **20 Day Job Search System** has worked for countless people who have connected with their ideal referrals and gained the biggest advantage they can have in their application process: **Someone at their target company vouching for them.** If you're looking for an Unfair Advantage that will set you apart in the final stages of your job search, this is it.

INTERVIEW WITHOUT THE STRESS

You've created the foundation of your job search, applied with confidence—knowing your resume is geared to pass the Applicant Tracking System—and have put yourself on the fast track to success by identifying those who will turn into your Ideal Referrals.

But to become "The One," you can't stop there. There's still one more key part of your job search to master if you want to truly outshine your final competition and be front-of-mind to your key decision-makers.

The Interview. Ahh, yes. Everyone's favorite part of their job search, right? WRONG! In fact, 93% of job seekers say they experience stress and nervousness before an interview.[2] Even more, statistics show that job interviews are second on the list of things that inherently make us the most nervous—just after public speaking—making it even worse than going on a first date![3]

But why? What's the REAL reason behind the stress we feel during the interview process, and is there a way to avoid it altogether?

Well, let me ask you this. "If you had an interview to prepare for right now, what would you do?"

---

2. "How Americans Prepare for Interviews," 2020, JDP, https://www.jdp.com/blog/how-to-prepare-for-interviews-2020. Extract: "It's no wonder an overwhelming majority of Americans—93 percent—have experienced anxiety related to job interviews."

3. "How Americans Prepare for Interviews," 2020, JDP, https://www.jdp.com/blog/how-to-prepare-for-interviews-2020. Extract: "In researching how candidates prepare for interviews, we found that only public speaking makes respondents more nervous than job interviews."

If your answer is similar to what mine used to be, you might find yourself Googling "The Most Asked Interview Questions," and then searching YouTube for answering tips and templates.

And, if you're like most people, even after all of this so-called "preparation," you still won't feel remotely prepared for the most important step of your job search.

Here's a harsh truth about the interview: It's the ONLY part of the job search where you don't have complete control. When it comes to your resume, LinkedIn, and networking, you have complete control over what you say and how you present yourself. But the interview is different, and that's why it is an ACHILLES HEEL for countless job seekers before and after you. Here's the thing: It doesn't have to be this way!

What if I told you that NOT having control of the interview was a false reality? Something taken as truth from an out-of-date process that puts you into an endless crazy cycle when you need confidence the most.

Yes, it's impossible to mind-read your interviewer and know every question you'll be asked in advance—and that's why COMPLETE control will never be an interview reality.

You see, control is lost because preparation is only focused on the things you CAN'T control—things like preparing for the exact questions you MIGHT be asked, and then trying to memorize and rehearse each answer.

As we begin to redefine the way you interview, I want you to remember this: You LOSE control when you prepare for WHAT questions you MIGHT be asked. And you GAIN control when you understand the process of HOW to answer any question you're asked.

I learned this the hard way when looking for my first post-college job and asking myself, "Why is this so complicated?" This question went continuously through my mind as I was on my FIFTH interview with no end in sight.

Things weren't going well, and each time I had a new interview I felt like I was putting myself through an endless cycle—a process that involved spending hours prepping for every possible question.

The result? I had even worse anxiety because deep down, even though I knew I had put in a TON of effort, I was still scared I'd be asked a question I hadn't prepared for.

In other words, it was a foundation built on a house of cards. One that wasn't just unique to me. And one that became even clearer to me as I started my journey as a consultant helping job seekers.

The thought of "It shouldn't be this complicated" came to my mind as professional after professional came to me totally stressed about past interview failures. But this time, I asked myself, "How can it be fixed?"

THE SOLUTION

To find an answer to this question, I spent hundreds of hours analyzing interview answers, testing different answering techniques (like PAR, STAR, etc.), and recording the most asked Interview Questions into a Spreadsheet to rank them based on how frequently they were asked.

However, with each new idea, the same results kept staring me in the face. The interview preparation process wasn't getting easier, and my clients weren't experiencing the lower stress levels and preparation times that I knew they deserved.

That's when I finally had an idea—one that I kicked myself for not thinking of earlier because I had, quite possibly, the best resource in front of me to find an answer to my question. One of my closest mentors and family friends, Aaron, had been a C-Suite HR Executive for over 15 years. Aaron had conducted thousands of interviews over his career encompassing just about any position and experience-level that existed.

Better yet, he is now an expert who focuses on training professionals in Effective Communication techniques—with a special emphasis on understanding two-way communication patterns that create positive, win-win results. I figured that he had to have an answer to my question, and sure enough, he did.

When I came to Aaron with my problem, his wheels immediately started to turn. In fact, we spent the next 4 hours on Zoom drawing out ideas on our whiteboards and diving deep into WHY the interview process had become such an insurmountable challenge. For Aaron, the core problem was easy to find. One that he noticed negatively impacted his experience with interviewers. And one that now was easy for him to identify because of his deep expertise in Effective Communication.

He said:

"Almost every interviewee thinks that if their response is what THEY want to hear, that it will positively resonate with the interviewer and leave a lasting impact. But this is not true. As interviewers, we are trained to look for specific criteria—precise experiences in the interviewer's past and self-insights about themselves that would have a positive direct impact on their future work team and our company.

Then, we look for them to give specific examples from their unique experience to prove the claims they initially make. At the end of the day, we want clear-cut proof that the interviewer fits into our team and can provide great value in the position for which they are interviewing.

Here's the thing though, Tommy. All the answering techniques out there miss the most important piece of the puzzle. They start their process focusing on the problem or situation—not with the ACTION they want the interviewer to take as a result of their answer. They never address the piece of the puzzle that actually prompts us to take action and have a positive emotional response."

Once Aaron said this, it really opened my eyes. As job seekers, we really were going about the interview process all wrong. Yes, identifying the situation or problem, and then communicating what action you took and what results you achieved are important—but the focus, and base of your answer, is all on YOU. Not the other way around, where the clear objective is to answer the question in a way that sparks the INTERVIEWER to take your desired action.

By shifting your focus to controlling the interviewer's action, you immediately re-establish control of your interview process. It's not a guessing game where you HOPE you are saying the right things, or that your experiences are enough to beat out other candidates. Instead, you're relying on an age-old communication technique that puts the power back into your hands—understanding what the other side is looking for, and then tailoring your answer to inspire action and belief.

This was a transformative moment for Aaron and me. The first step in any interviewee's response pattern had to start with the ACTION they wanted the interviewer to take. Then from there, they had to spark BELIEF with specific experiences from their professional history and provide PROOF with the correlated results from those experiences.

This is where our AnswerIQ Pyramid was born. The interview response framework that has changed the game for thousands of job seekers and given them a clear answering path for ANY interview question they're asked.

THE ANSWERIQ PYRAMID

Starting as a simple sketch on a whiteboard, we built the AnswerIQ Pyramid to take you through the mental thought process needed to hook your interview audiences with the right answers.

The AnswerIQ Pyramid is the ultimate interview response tool because it provides you the proven answering structure you need but also centers around the desired outcome you want the INTERVIEWER to take, not what YOU want to say.

In the next three sections in this chapter, I'll explore the following three "levels" in the pyramid:

- The top of the pyramid: the ACTION level.

- The middle of the pyramid: the INSIGHT level.

- The bottom of the pyramid: the EXPLANATION level.

QUESTION

[Pyramid diagram:
- Top: **Action** — DO — "What do I want the interviewer to do?"
- Middle: **Insights** (CLAIM) — BELIEVE — "What does the interviewer need to believe in order to take action?"
- Bottom: **Explanation** (PROVE) — KNOW — "How do I prove it to be true?" (FROM JOB SEEKER DNA & RESUME)
- Arrow labeled INSIGHT PATH connects Explanation up to Insights]

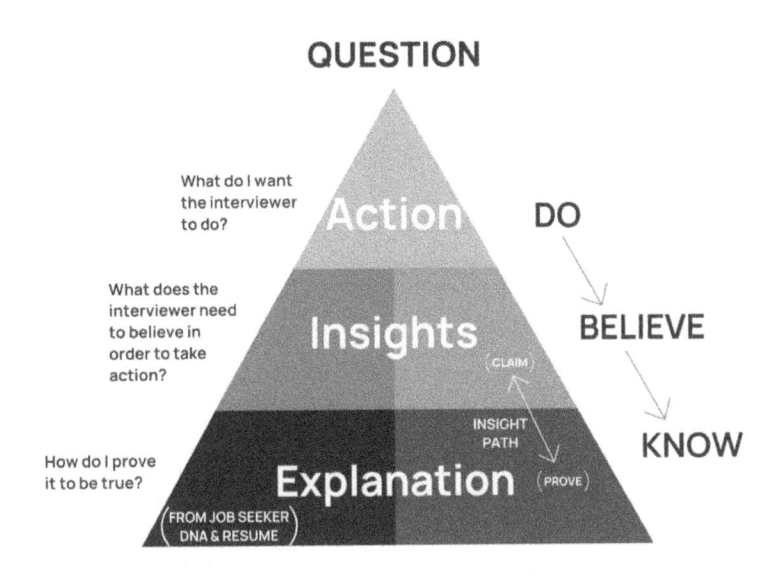

THE ACTION LEVEL

To get started and see how this AnswerIQ Pyramid tool will change the way you interview and effectively communicate forever, let's begin at the very top: **The Action Level.**

As soon as you're asked an interview question, you need to ask yourself, **"As a result of my answer, what do I want the interviewer to do?"**

You see, all great communication begins with inspiring ACTION. And to achieve that, you first need to view your response through the eyes of your audience—which in this case is the interviewer.

And by asking yourself what you want the interviewer to do before forming your answer, you now have the theme and purpose you can use to hit their major pain points and respond to their question in a way that gives the interviewer the exact information they crave.

It's this change of perspective, and beginning your process of thinking about the END RESULT first that will get your answer started on the right path.

And remember: It's important to be specific. The more specific you are with the action, the easier everything else becomes. Your interviewer won't take the action you want them to take simply because you want them to take it. They will ONLY take action if there's some motivation or reason for them to do so.

THE INSIGHT LEVEL

This brings us to the next level of the Pyramid, and also the most important in your answering process: **The Insight Level**—where you'll explore WHAT causes your audience to take action.

Here's an example to best explain this: Let's say you're thinking of applying for two different jobs:

- The first job has a high number of applicants, has been posted for 3 weeks, and is a position that would be slightly out of your experience level.

- The second job was posted less than 24 hours ago, has only 2 applicants, and is a strong fit for both your experience level and natural skills.

Which position would you feel the most confident applying for? If you chose the second job, you just uncovered the secret behind WHAT causes people to take action—it's BELIEF.

In analyzing both jobs side-by-side, there were 3 things you needed to believe before you chose the best opportunity:

- You had a higher chance of getting the second job due to being an initial applicant.

- You had fewer candidates to compete against.

- Your skills and experience for the second opportunity positioned you as a strong fit and high-level candidate.

Makes sense, right? Those 3 ideas led to your ultimate decision, and this example proves that the establishment of those beliefs led you to take the appropriate action.

Which brings us to the most crucial question you should ask yourself when forming a response, **"What does the interviewer need to BELIEVE to take the desired action?"**

Those beliefs are your answer's big ideas—or as we like to call them, INSIGHTS. And insights don't come from hope, meditation, or out of thin air—they come from centering your answer on what your interviewer needs to BELIEVE rather than what YOU want to say.

So, if insight leads to action, what leads to insight? That answer is actually quite simple: It's KNOWLEDGE, which comes from how you explain the material found in the 2 main content sources job seekers create in my system—their Job Seeker DNA Report and Resume.

THE EXPLANATION LEVEL

Which leads us to the bottom level of your Pyramid—**The Explanation Level**—where you'll PROVE your insights to be true.

Big ideas must be supported, and without any supporting knowledge, an insight is merely a CLAIM. For instance, if you answered the interview question, "What are your greatest strengths" by saying, "I'm a great communicator and work well with others in teams," then you're only giving a CLAIM—not a proven answer with examples to back it up.

And that's why when you answer an interview question, you always need to ask yourself, **"How do I PROVE this to be true?"**

So, now that we've gone through each layer of the AnswerIQ Pyramid, let's put it into action with, most likely, the very FIRST question you'll be asked in your interview. **"Tell me about yourself."**

If you were asked this question right now in an interview, your first goal would be to determine what you want to achieve with your response. The desired ACTION you want the interviewer to take is to gain a better understanding of your background to consider you as a strong candidate for the job.

Once you've identified what you want the interviewer to DO, this would then lead you to the Insights Level of the Pyramid— where you'll identify the big ideas that would convince the interviewer you're the right candidate for the job.

So, in this example, here are the 3 Insights you could have CLAIMED to lead your interviewer to the desired action.

Insight 1: I have the capability of handling multiple activities at once and am a talented, creative, problem solver.

Insight 2: My professional history showcases a consistent pattern of delivering results and meeting organizational objectives.

Insight 3: I'm dedicated to personal growth and professional development, always seeking to expand my knowledge and expertise.

Then, after writing your claims down, the next step is PROVING them to be true with concrete evidence and examples, all sourced from the Professional Experience section on your resume.

And as you can see from the AnswerIQ Pyramid, that's exactly what happens in the Explanation Level.

For Insight 1: At XYZ Company, I successfully orchestrated a cross-platform marketing strategy while simultaneously troubleshooting app interface issues. This led to a 20% increase in user engagement.

For Insight 2: At ABC Corp., I spearheaded a project that brought in a 15% increase in revenue within the first quarter of its launch.

For Insight 3: Recently, I completed a course on Data Analytics which I used at my last job to save $20,000 in annual advertising expenses.

Now, it's time for the final response—which you can form at the bottom of your Pyramid.

Thank you for the opportunity to introduce myself. Throughout my career as a/an [Industry] Professional, I've always thrived in roles that demanded versatility and multitasking.

For instance, in my previous position at XYZ Company, I managed complex marketing campaigns while simultaneously collaborating with the tech team to integrate our promotions into the app interface. This really required me to balance both my creativity and analytical thinking.

In one memorable instance, I led a cross-platform marketing strategy while also addressing app interface challenges—which led to a 20% uptick in user engagement.

Beyond that, over the past 5 years, I've taken the lead on three major projects—with each coming in under budget and ahead of schedule. At ABC Corp., I was particularly proud of a project that resulted in a 15% revenue increase within its first quarter.

And lastly, I'm deeply committed to continuous learning. I hold certifications in both Project Management and Digital Marketing, and I regularly attend workshops to stay at the forefront of industry trends.

Recently after completing a Data Analytics course, I leveraged those new skills to optimize our advertising budget in my last role, saving the company 10%.

I believe these skills and experiences make me a valuable addition to any team, and I'm eager to bring this same dedication and drive to your organization.

THIS is the right way to answer the "Tell me about yourself" question. Your key decision-makers aren't looking to hear about your favorite weekend hobbies or your favorite place to eat. Save that for your friends and family!

Your key decision-makers are looking for a quick snapshot into WHY they should choose you for the job. It's your ability to effectively communicate your unique value that will set you apart from other candidates, and the AnswerIQ Pyramid was specifically built to take you through the mental thought pattern needed to hook the key decision-makers in your interview process.

Just remember this before moving on: Your response, and the exact wording you use, will be different every time you practice this question, including when you answer it during your interview—and that's totally FINE.

Think about this: We can't even write our names precisely the same way twice—I'm serious, try it. We weren't meant to be perfect, repetitive robots, and that's where memorization can be the biggest downfall in the interview preparation process.

The purpose of the AnswerIQ Pyramid is to get you OUT of that box and teach you HOW to answer the question.

So, now that we've worked through the AnswerIQ Pyramid to form a response, you may be thinking, "Okay Tommy, that's great, but it seems like a long thought process. How would I actually use this to quickly form answers in the heat of the interview?"

First and foremost, the more times you use the AnswerIQ Pyramid for practice, the quicker your mind will begin to form pathways that lead directly to your responses.

Second, when you go through the full InterviewIQ Training in our system, you will learn the two shorthand response versions of the AnswerIQ Pyramid to use that will equip you to reply in the heat of the interview in just SECONDS.

This is how you permanently eliminate the stress and anxiety that comes from interviewing. It's not through hours of memorization or learning hundreds of questions you could be asked. It's by knowing HOW to answer any question that comes your way.

Remember, there is no substitute for practice. Benjamin Franklin said this best in his famous quote: "By failing to prepare, you are preparing to fail."

Practice is what separates the few from many, and if you want to land your dream job, the extra effort you put in now WILL separate you from the competition and get you REMEMBERED by your key decision-makers.

CAREER COMMANDERS ASSIGNMENT

For your Career Commanders Assignment for this chapter, I want you to work through your own AnswerIQ Pyramid and form your response to the "Tell me about yourself" statement. Then either post your reply in the Career Commanders Community or, for extra credit, take a short video of yourself responding to the question and share it with your peers.

Remember, there are key decision-makers in our community and an entire recruiter network looking for a candidate just like you—**the Obvious Candidate.**

Yes, by investing the time to go through this book, doing the Career Commanders Assignments, and gaining clarity around how to land your dream job and get paid more to do it, you now know exactly what it takes to become **the Obvious Candidate.**

You know that the job search process doesn't need to take an average of 5 months when you have the RIGHT system that works for you.

You've learned how to complete the Dream Job Formula by gaining a profound understanding of yourself and your 4 key decision-makers.

You've gained an Unfair Advantage in knowing how to use your resume—the number one marketing tool in your job search arsenal—to HOOK your key decision-makers across your entire job search, no matter your experience level or expertise.

On LinkedIn, you've turned "on" the N'sider Settings to get instantly noticed and attract recruiters and hiring managers like a magnet.

You've received the GOLDEN TICKET in your job search and can help ensure your resume passes the Applicant Tracking System at your top opportunities.

And you know how to WIN the final stages of your job search and become "The One" who stands out over your competitors and lands the job.

Your dream job is just around the corner!

Now, I just have one more question. "If you could add thousands to your final salary without risking the job, would you do it?"

Of course, right?! I'm here to help you take command of your career and put the power back into your hands. If you're ready to leave fear at the door and experience the final and most rewarding part of your job search, turn the page for literal FREE MONEY!

CHAPTER 7: HOW TO ADD THOUSANDS TO YOUR FINAL SALARY

"*I know I deserve more than this. I've worked too hard to get where I am to just settle.*"

These were the first words Ethan said to me over the phone when he hired me to help him in his job search process. Having trudged through 8 years of medical school with his life-long goal of being a Pharmacist on the horizon, Ethan was ready to see his years of hard work and patience finally pay off.

He had a problem, though, and it wasn't getting job offers. Because of his status as a first-year Pharmacist, Ethan was not being presented with a salary that he believed reflected his achievements in med school, or the average starting salary of his peers who went to the same prestigious school.

Yes, location could be playing a factor, as he was settling his roots in a smaller town than most of his classmates, but he still believed that he could do better. And he was right!

When Ethan and I sat down to identify his unique market value, we found that his current level of expertise and skills most definitely did require a salary higher than what he was receiving. In fact, he was being undervalued by potential employers by an average of $10,000. No wonder he felt under-appreciated!

Now, this was obviously a large discrepancy, so I asked Ethan the reaction of his interested companies when he countered with a higher salary after they provided their initial, low offer, and I'll never forget the look on his face. Ethan said, "Wait, I can do that? No way, they would get offended and I would lose my opportunity altogether."

That sounds like a pretty logical statement, right? The company has their determined salary for the position, there are probably other candidates competing for the same role, and if you ask for more money, they will just move on and offer it to the candidate who will accept that salary.

On the surface, it seems like reality—but it's NOT! In fact, it couldn't be further from the truth.

KNOW YOUR WORTH

I want to ask you the same question I asked Ethan when working with him that day. "If you knew in advance that you could ask for more money WITHOUT any penalties, and the chance of you getting that money was extremely high, would you do it?"

Now, you're probably giving me the same response he did, "Of course I would Tommy, that's a silly question."

But here's the truth. This is the EXACT scenario you'll find yourself in when you have a job offer on the table—and I don't want you to be like the 70% of other job seekers who let FEAR cost them THOUSANDS of dollars.[1]

This doesn't just happen to Ethan. It happens to MILLIONS of job seekers every year, and it happened to me when going through my own job search process, too.

---

1. Kathleen Elkins, "71% of employees are missing out on a simple way to earn more money," CNBC, May 2017, https://www.cnbc.com/2017/05/25/most-employees-dont-negotiate-their-salary.html Note: this CNBC article quotes the following study by Jobvite: "Job SeekerNation Study: Finding the Fault Lines in the American Workforce," May 2017, https://www.jobvite.com/wp-content/uploads/2017/05/2017_Job_Seeker_Nation_Survey.pdf

You see, I was guilty of letting my fear get the best of me—and I wondered why in the world I would risk all my hard work when there was the certainty of a new job on the table. But as it turned out, I didn't know how wrong I was.

They always say timing is everything, and that couldn't have been more true for me as I was in the middle of a Business Strategy night class while pursuing my Master's Degree.

To give some context, I was 5 months into my job search and finally had my golden ticket—a concrete offer on the table. But there was a problem: It was a salary of $7,000 lower than what I expected to be paid.

And due to my frustration, I complained about it A LOT that night to my group. My venting really reached a tipping point, though, when Dan—the group's quietest member—said, "Why don't you just ask for more?" Shocked and confused, I said, "Yeah right, and lose this opportunity to someone who WILL accept that salary?"

But what Dan said next changed everything.

He said, "No, you don't understand. I've worked in HR for 6 years, and we NEVER give our top dollar amount in the first offer. In fact, we EXPECT people to negotiate their salary and leave ourselves room in the budget to do so."

As soon as he said this, it felt like an "aha" moment for me.

Of course they would leave room in the budget—because for them, the offer isn't PERSONAL like it is for me. Instead, it's a business decision that ultimately reflects the bottom line.

And after picking Dan's brain for a few hours later that night, I felt confident enough to counter-offer the next day.

Now, it definitely wasn't perfect—and knowing what I know today, I could have received even MORE money—but I did successfully end up getting that extra $7,000. Just as importantly, when I counter-offered, the company DID NOT give the job to someone else.

As with anything, though, I needed to make sure that Dan's intel—and my situation—weren't outliers. So before I started passing this knowledge on to others. I spoke with every HR Manager and Payroll Specialist I knew. I even cold messaged several on LinkedIn.

And guess what? They all said the SAME thing. After going INSIDE the company and forming relationships with the key decision-makers who control salary, 3 truths began to emerge.

The same truths that helped me add thousands to my final salary. The same truths that have helped thousands since then get paid more to do their dream jobs. And the same truths that helped Ethan ultimately negotiate a final salary that was over $10,000 MORE than his initial offer! Just look at what he had to say about the experience.

"I had just graduated from medical school and was close to reaching my life-long goal of becoming a Pharmacist, but I didn't just want to take any job. I wanted a salary that matched the hard work and years I'd put into my education. But the offers I was getting weren't quite hitting the mark. That's when I decided to bring Tommy on board to help me with my negotiation strategy, and I'm so glad I did!

Tommy changed everything I knew about the negotiation process and opened my eyes to how it actually works. And not only that, he helped me find my market value, my exact counter-offer percentage, and then custom-tailored an entire negotiation playbook just for me! I was able to leverage my offers, provide a counter-offer to my top company, and accept their final offer that was over $10,000 MORE than their initial offer! It's exactly what I knew I was worth!

Tommy turned my fear of negotiation into a huge win. Thanks to him, I'm starting my career on the right foot and at the right pay. I can't recommend Tommy and his system enough!"

Here are the 3 Offer Truths that will add THOUSANDS to your final salary.

OFFER TRUTH 1

Offer Truth 1: Your Initial Salary is NOT the Company's Top Offer.

While you may think the offer from your target company was a dream come true, the reality is that it was NOT at the top end of what they could pay you. Chances are, they didn't even offer you the midpoint.

You see, the job search is a high-stakes, extremely personal process for you—but to the company, hiring and determining salary is old news and very impersonal.

Think about it. The recruiter or hiring manager isn't offering you THEIR money. Also, the accounting department that creates the budget isn't using personal assets.

And at the end of the day, your salary is simply another number in their system—part of a larger structure that's used as a guideline for offers and negotiations. But the great news is that you can use all of this to your advantage. You just need to know the hidden secrets I learned from going deep inside this process.

So, are you ready to hear the two factors that will change how you view your salary forever?

Well, it all comes down to **Pay Grades** and **Pay Scales**. Yes, we explored these in chapter 1, but they're so essential that I'm going to go even deeper into them in this chapter.

Almost every company uses a **Pay Grade System**—which associates a certain minimum and maximum salary range with specific positions.

And in many cases, Pay Grades are given a certain designated label and are mapped to positions of the same level across the organization—hence the term "That's above my Pay Grade."

When a company breaks down their **Pay Grades** even further, they link them to **Pay Scales**—which are the minimum, midpoint, and maximum annual salaries within a specific Pay Grade.

In the following example, I've listed 8 Pay Grades, each with 3 dollar amounts that correspond to the minimum salary, midpoint salary, and a maximum salary.

- Pay Grade 1: Receptionist: $25,000 / $35,000 / $45,000.

- Pay Grade 2: Customer Support Associate: $30,000 / $35,000 / $40,000.

- Pay Grade 3: Digital Marketing Coordinator: $40,000 / $50,000 / $60,000.

- Pay Grade 4: Project Coordinator: $50,000 / $60,000 / $70,000.

- Pay Grade 5: Senior Data Analyst: $70,000 / $90,000 / $110,000.

- Pay Grade 6: Sales Manager: $90,000 / $110,000 / $130,000.

- Pay Grade 7: Financial Controller: $120,000 / $150,000 / $180,000.

- Pay Grade 8: Chief Operations Officer: $180,000 / $250,000 / $350,000.

When it comes to your salary negotiation, the Pay Scale will be the base on which your strategy is built. While you may not be able to change the Pay Grade of your specific role, you CAN change where you sit on its Pay Scale. That is, instead of getting the minimum salary or midpoint salary, you can get the maximum salary.

OFFER TRUTH 2

Offer Truth 2: Companies Find Their Pay Scales The Same Way You Do.

The offer you received from your target company wasn't made from thin air—and the same thing can be said about your position's salary structure.

Just as you'll learn how to do salary research to calculate your Market Value a little later in this chapter, companies research what their competitors are paying employees in your same position.

And here's the secret: The tools companies use to determine their Pay Scales are almost IDENTICAL to the ones that you'll use to find your Market Value. The only difference is that you can find yours for FREE.

You see, by simply looking at various REAL data points for your position, you can form a midpoint that closely resembles that of your target company and know how much room you have to maneuver up the Pay Scale.

OFFER TRUTH 3

Offer Truth 3: Companies Anticipate Negotiation.

There's a reason why your initial offer is NEVER the company's top offer. They EXPECT you to negotiate—and leave themselves room for you to do so.

And just as much as you want to MAKE money, they want to SAVE money. So, what's the best way for them to do that? Well, it certainly isn't going higher and higher—or even by starting at their midpoint.

Their strategy is to start as low as possible in your Pay Scale and then work up through negotiation.

They believe that by starting low, there's a good chance the final amount will still be around the midpoint—meaning they successfully did their jobs and saved on payroll expenses.

But here's what they're NOT expecting: For you to know your EXACT Market Value and the Leverage you have over the situation.

Now, as I've prioritized throughout this entire book, I don't just want to talk about my system. I want to SHOW you my system and how it can instantly start working for you in your own job search.

That's why in our exercise for this chapter, you're going to lay the foundation for your negotiation process and learn how to calculate your exact Market Value.

Just don't forget this: Whether you have a job offer on the table right now, or will have one in the near future, NEVER skip this step—even if you think you have a dollar amount in mind.

In fact, if you ignore the process it takes to calculate your Market Value, you'll never find the Leverage you need to counter your initial offer successfully—and as a result, you could lose out on up to 20% of your potential pay.

So, that raises the question: "If Market Value is the key to unlocking Leverage, and Leverage is what gives you control over your Negotiation Process, how can you identify your Market Value BEFORE you need to give your Counter Offer?"

Well, the answer can be found in your PREDICTED Pay Scale—the range that takes the TANGIBLE, such as identifying your range of pay with proven salary aggregators, and merges in with the INTANGIBLE—which we'll do through something we call "Unbiased Comparison."

By the way, if you haven't heard of salary aggregators before, they're just a website that collects and compiles salary data from various sources, such as job postings, company websites, and government databases.

FINDING YOUR PREDICTED PAY SCALE DATA USING SALARY.COM

The first salary aggregator tool we'll use to find data for your Predicted Pay Scale is Salary.com.

Here's what you should do:

- Go to Salary.com's homepage.
- Find the "What Am I Worth" box.
- Enter your desired Job Title.
- Enter your Location.
- Click "Get My Salary Estimate."

Salary.com will show you search results for various job descriptions that relate to the one you entered. For instance, if you entered Account Manager as your desired Job Title, then Salary.com would have shown you a bunch of related positions, including:

- Account Manager I.
- Account Manager II.
- Account Manager III.

- Account Manager IV.

- Account Management Manager.

- Account Relationship Manager.

- Channel Account Manager.

Scroll through the results on your screen, and select the job description that best matches your situation. If there are some Roman numerals at the end of some Job Descriptions, know that these numbers differentiate between various levels of experience: the lower the Roman numeral, the more junior the role; the higher the Roman numeral, the more senior the role.

After you've selected a position, you'll be taken to a Job Page. The first thing you'll see is a Bell Curve which represents the combination of thousands of salary data points from real positions at real companies that correspond to your Job Description.

Your objective is to use this Bell Curve to figure out the Predicted Pay Scale that your company is using. To achieve that, you'll want to find the Minimum, Midpoint, and Maximum salaries for your position. To accomplish that, look at the data in the Bell Curve and realize that:

- The 10% mark can be thought of as the Minimum.

- The 50% mark can be thought of as the Midpoint.

- The 90% mark can be thought of as the Maximum.

- (It's best to ignore salaries that are below the 10% mark or above the 90% mark because they skew the data.)

So, for example, if you searched for an Account Manager I position located in Omaha, Nebraska, here would be your Predicted Pay Scale:

- $46,550 is the Minimum (which represents what the lowest 10% of Account Manager I positions are paid in that location).

- $60,830 is the Midpoint (which represents the median salary for Account Manager I positions at that location).

- $80,380 is the Maximum (which represents the highest 90% of Account Manager I positions at that location).

To get even more accurate insights into your Pay Scale, enter in additional information below the Bell Curve, including:

- Your education.

- Your years of experience.

- Your number of direct reports.

- The people you reported to.

- And your performance.

After you've input this extra information, look at the Minimum, Maximum, and Midpoint values again, and write them down. You'll use these figures in an averaging exercise later on.

FINDING YOUR PREDICTED PAY SCALE DATA USING GLASSDOOR.COM

Now head over to Glassdoor.com, another leading source for salary information.

Here's what you should do:

- Go to Glassdoor.com's homepage.
- Click the "Salaries" tab.
- Find the box titled, "Are you paid fairly? Find out."
- Enter your desired Job Title.
- Enter your Location.
- Click the search button.

Glassdoor.com will show you a page that is very similar to the page you just saw at Salary.com. This time, though, instead of a Bell Curve, you'll see a Bar Chart.

Add additional information to further refine the search results:

- Your years of experience.

- Your industry.

After you've entered that information, on the left, notice the following three figures:

- Total Pay Range.

- Base Pay.

- Additional Pay.

Here's the important part: We only want to consider Base Pay. You can pretty much ignore the Total Pay figure because it includes things like cash bonuses, stock bonuses, profit sharing, sales commissions, and tips—all things that can vary and usually aren't reflected in your initial offer.

To find your true Pay Scale range, subtract the Additional Pay from the lowest and highest data points in the "Most Likely Range" of the chart. That will give you your Minimum and Maximum numbers. When you have those two Minimum and Maximum figures, calculate their average, which will give you the Midpoint figure.

AVERAGE YOUR SALARY.COM AND GLASSDOOR.COM FIGURES

To find your overall Predicted Pay Scale, take the figures from both Salary.com and Glassdoor.com, and average each of them. In other words:

- Calculate the average of the two Minimum numbers.

- Calculate the average of the two Midpoint numbers.

- Calculate the average of the two Maximum numbers.

Using these two aggregator tools is going to give you the most accurate representation you can find when calculating your Predicted Pay Scale and seeing where you fit within it.

THE UNBIASED COMPARISON EXERCISE

The next step in identifying where you fit within your Predicted Pay Scale is to use the **Unbiased Comparison Exercise.**

To achieve this, you'll measure yourself against the average person doing YOUR job in YOUR target company—which can be identified by using your Predicted Midpoint from your Predicted Pay Scale.

Once you have your Midpoint, there are three main comparison factors you must consider when determining your EXACT Market Value.

- Your Education Level.

- Your Depth of Experience.

- Your Relevant Skills and Competencies.

Now, trying to be as unbiased and objective as possible, I want you to think about your three above areas, and compare yourself to your position's job description. In each of three above areas, ask yourself if you're under-qualified, qualified, or over-qualified. Your three questions are:

- Does my education level make me under-qualified, qualified, or over-qualified for this job?

- Does my experience make me under-qualified, qualified, or over-qualified for this job?

- Do my skills and competencies make me under-qualified, qualified, or over-qualified for this job?

Based on your answers, you can adjust your Midpoint up or down to reflect the value you bring in comparison to the average person doing your job. This new figure can be thought of as your NEW Market Value.

WHAT'S YOUR NEXT MOVE?

Now that you know HOW companies structure their pay and WHERE you fit within your position's Pay Scale, what's next? How can you turn your newfound Market Value into actual money? Hint: keep reading and in the next chapter I'll show you how to create a WIN-WIN scenario for both you and your target company every time.

There's one final thought I'd like to share before we close this chapter. I want you to leave your FEAR at the door. Sure, salary negotiation can be intimidating, and that's why it's been so important to me to share these 3 Offer Truths with you.

So keep them in mind as you implement the value and insights you've gained throughout this book into your job search process. Because as the old saying goes, "Everything you want is on the other side of fear."

It's time to get off the sidelines and take ACTION! So keep reading because in the next chapter, I'm going to reveal my secret sauce that has helped thousands go from frustrated job seekers to Career Commanders faster than any job search solution in history—and I'm going to GIVE it to you!

CHAPTER 8: A SPECIAL SURPRISE FOR YOU!

Frustrated Job Seekers | Career Commanders

Secret Sauce

THE SECRET SAUCE

Before we get into the heart of this chapter, I want to ask you a question. "Are you ready to get an Unfair Advantage so strong that it will change the entire trajectory of your career?" I ask this with seriousness. Some people are afraid of change. The status quo is what's normal to them, and they are fine with sub-par results.

But I know that's not you. If it was, you wouldn't still be reading this book. You're someone who's committed to taking action, gaining superior results, and being in COMMAND of your CAREER.

For that reason, I have something I'm SUPER excited to share with you! Remember when I said that if you read this entire book, I had a special surprise for you? Well, this has been something I've been holding in since the very first chapter of this book because it IS the secret sauce that makes finding your dream job truly possible.

As you know, I created this book for you to:

- Have a clear vision of your Dream Job.

- Know EXACTLY what it takes to land it in Days, not Months.

And I know both of those goals have become a reality by investing the time and implementing the Career Commanders Exercises into your job search.

But, you may have been asking yourself questions like:

- "What if I want MORE than just clarity?"

- "What if I want the step-by-step system to follow that eliminates all the guesswork, does all the hard work FOR me, and takes me straight to my dream job?"

Well, if you're asking those kinds of questions—or have been wondering what makes our system different from anything else you've ever seen before—I'm going to show you NOW.

This is the EXACT System I've created that has our job seekers finding, landing, and thriving in their dream jobs faster than any other job search solution in history.

CHOICES

Now, you have a choice. You can either keep going through your job search all by yourself. OR, you can trust me as your guide and choose to follow a system that's specially designed to be your ultimate assistant throughout each step of your job search process. This is a choice only you can make.

When considering your choice, ask yourself the following:

- Isn't it time I landed the job I truly desire and deserve?

- Isn't it time to take command over my career and put the power back in my hands?

- Isn't it time to step out of my comfort zone and go after my wildest dreams?

- If I don't do this now, when will I take that step?

I would encourage you to have faith, trust your gut, and remember that the most SUCCESSFUL people are those who take ACTION. They know that if they don't take action now, there might not ever be a LATER.

We're not guaranteed unlimited time on earth. We all have an expiration date, and I would suggest and encourage you to make the most of your time by doing what it takes to land the job of your dreams with our system as your guide!

THE 20 DAY JOB SEARCH PROGRAM

I invite you to join the program I've created called **The 20 Day Job Search.** The first and only job search system built to give you a total UNFAIR ADVANTAGE across each stage of your search process! In it, you'll become a true Career Commander.

I created this program so you don't have to go through the unnecessary stress, rejection, and failures that I, myself, and MILLIONS of other job seekers have gone through before you.

I want you to completely AVOID all that pain, okay? In fact, it's my mission to ensure no other job seeker ever has to get trapped in that crazy cycle again.

THIS PROGRAM IS NOT FOR YOU IF …

The **20 Day Job Search** program is NOT for you if you'd rather work HARDER than SMARTER.

This is NOT for you if you're not interested in doing the RIGHT work necessary to REALLY make your dreams become reality.

And this is NOT for you if you think that investing in the BEST training on how to find your dream job is an EXPENSE, rather than an INVESTMENT that changes your entire career trajectory and gives you back MONTHS of salary.

THIS PROGRAM IS PERFECT FOR YOU IF ...

On the flip side, The **20 Day Job Search** program is PERFECT for you if you're tired of trying to put bits and pieces of this together by yourself—such as how to craft a resume and LinkedIn Profile that makes you the MOST Obvious Candidate, or manually sifting through and guessing WHY your applications are falling through the cracks.

This is PERFECT for you if you want the exact roadmap for the New Way of Job Searching.

And this is PERFECT for you if you want a GIANT shortcut to landing your DREAM JOB.

TESTIMONIAL: ERIC

Remember Eric's story that I shared in a previous chapter? He could create amazing products that sold like clockwork, but when it came to his own job search, he didn't know how to sell himself and was following poor advice. In other words, his chances of landing his dream job were close to zero.

But when Eric came across my **20 Day Job Search** Program, it was as if all the lights came on. He had a system that took on all the heavy lifting, cleared up confusion, and gave him a clear path to become the MOST Obvious Candidate.

And as a result, he didn't just find ANY OLD job. He landed the job he truly deserved—and he did so in just 18 DAYS, before he even completed the entire program!

And when you follow the RIGHT system, this is totally possible for you, too!

WHAT'S IN THE 20 DAY JOB SEARCH PROGRAM?

The 20 Day Job Search program includes 8 easy-to-follow TRAINING MODULES that are all 100% delivered by me, Tommy West. And each one of these training modules is one part of the all-inclusive system we've created.

The training modules can be consumed at your own pace. Yes, the system is designed for you to have multiple interviews lined up and potential offers on the table at the end of these 20 Days—but that's only with a very minimal time commitment each day. You can actually move through it much quicker, and many of our job seekers do!

Each module is backed by our **Dream Job Formula** which, as I'm sure you'll remember from previous chapters, is a blend of the following core pieces that set my system apart from anything else:

- ACTIONABLE GUIDANCE that eliminates all the guesswork and shows you EXACTLY what to do.

- Our proprietary RESOURCE GUIDES that do all the hard work FOR you.

- The exclusive, corporate-level TOOLS that trim MONTHS off your job search and put the power directly back into your hands.

- And at its foundation, YOU—helping you become the MOST Obvious Candidate for each one of your dream opportunities.

I created **The 20 Day Job Search Program** so that ANYONE at any level of their career can simply go through it step-by-step and experience success. Let me show you how.

TRAINING MODULE 1: JOB SEEKER DNA

In the *Job Seeker DNA* module, you'll get access to our DNA Report Tool and Job Seeker Profile. With these, you'll learn how to communicate the intangible, indescribable parts of you across your ENTIRE job search. In doing so, you'll prime your path for becoming the Obvious Candidate.

TRAINING MODULE 2: RESUME MASTERY

In the *Resume Mastery* module, I'll provide you with our Ultimate Resume Blueprint, which will teach you how to write each part of your resume—leaving no question unanswered and ensuring it never gets lost in the mix again. I'll also give you instant access to our exclusive, corporate-sponsored PowerMyResume Tool to bring your resume to life and ensure it is "application ready."

TRAINING MODULE 3: LINKEDIN N'SIDER

In the **LinkedIn N'sider** module, you'll go through our Profile N'sider Masterclass. In it, I'll dive even deeper into the creation of each specific part of your LinkedIn Profile Page and the N'sider Settings you need to BEAT the LinkedIn Recruiter algorithm to cast a spotlight on yourself that recruiters and hiring managers can't miss.

TRAINING MODULE 4: SEARCH TACTICIAN

In the **Search Tactician** module, I'll show you the only 2 job boards you need to find EVERY single opportunity and then uncover the secret setting that brings you jobs on autopilot before any other candidate. No more wasting countless hours endlessly browsing random job boards and getting lost in all the mess.

TRAINING MODULE 5: ATS HACKER

In the **ATS Hacker** module, for the first time ever, I'll give you UNLIMITED access to our Application Master Key Tool that shows you the EXACT keywords you're missing for each of your job applications AND give you the Cheat Codes to automate the entire revisions process and pump out "ATS-Certified" Resumes in minutes.

Remember how I've said the job search process is built for COMPANIES, not for you? Well, being an early job applicant won't mean anything if your resume doesn't pass the

Applicant Tracking System (ATS), which is why I'm giving you this tool to get past each company's ATS.

TRAINING MODULE 6: NETWORKING MAGIC

In the Networking Magic module, I'll show you how to instantly find THOUSANDS of your ideal referrals without ever needing to speak with them in person. You'll get the Random Outsider to Instant Insider Toolkit. This toolkit contains our Ideal Referral Roadmap, The 3 P's Video Workshop, AND our Messaging Manual—The Done-for-You Guide that provides engaging, fill-in-the-blank scripts for every networking situation while saving you precious time.

TRAINING MODULE 7: INTERVIEWIQ

In the *InterviewIQ* module, you'll completely transform your job interview experience.

First, you'll learn how to avoid the number one mistake employers say candidates make in interviews.

Then, you'll uncover the 10 Universal Questions on which EVERY SINGLE interview question is based.

Next, you'll get our first-ever answering framework designed specifically for YOU, the interviewer, to help you respond INSTANTLY in the heat of the interview.

Lastly, you'll get our Ultimate Interview Survival Guide that has everything you need to have a stress-free experience.

TRAINING MODULE 8: THE FINISH LINE

In *The Finish Line* module, you'll use all your newfound expertise to take ACTION and apply for 3-5 of your dream opportunities per day, for each of the last 4 days of the course.

That means that, by the end of **the 20 Day Job Search Program**, you will have sent out 12-20 applications where you're positioned to be in the very TOP group of candidates. This will make it extremely likely that, at the VERY LEAST, you'll have several interviews lined up where you're primed to get an offer.

I designed **the 20 Day Job Search Program** to provide you with EVERYTHING you need to succeed in not JUST your job search, but in your career as a whole. Because when you know HOW to find a job and set yourself apart from any other candidate, you bulletproof yourself and take complete COMMAND over your entire CAREER.

That's why, as a Career Commander, I give you **Lifetime Access** to EVERYTHING in the Program. That includes all the video training, resource guides, exclusive tools, and all future updates that come with it.

WHAT BONUSES DO YOU GET IN THE 20 DAY JOB SEARCH PROGRAM?

While you might rightly expect that a system such as my **20 Day Job Search Program** would sell for around $5,000, I don't even want to tell you the website yet to sign up for it—because as a reader of this book, you're not going to be paying anywhere CLOSE to that price. And I still have several amazing FREE bonuses that you'll get when you sign up for my **20 Day Job Search Program**.

FREE BONUS 1: THE MASTER NEGOTIATOR COURSE

You'll get access to *The Master Negotiator Bonus Module.* In this bonus module, I'll show you WHY companies are intentionally leaving money on the table when they give your initial offer. And then, you'll get our Negotiator's Game Plan where you'll learn how to calculate an exact counter-offer and create a WIN-WIN scenario that adds THOUSANDS to your final salary. I'll also give you our All-in-One Negotiation Guide, which is packed full of money-making secrets and formulas.

FREE BONUS 2: COVER LETTER BLUEPRINT TRAINING

You'll get our *Cover Letter Blueprint Training.*

You see, while most job seekers think the Cover Letter is a relic of the past, it's still actually the Main Differentiator in the Final Stages of Your Job Search.

And in this Bonus, I'm not just going to give you immediate access to the Blueprint Training, I'm also going to give you the 5 Plug n' Play Cover Letters we use to help you instantly send out your applications, saving you countless hours of work.

FREE BONUS 3: THE BONUS CHEAT CODES

Then, the Third Missing Link you're going to get is FREE Bonus #3: *The Bonus Cheat Codes*—where I'll train you how to use our Application Master Key Tool to ensure your cover letters and LinkedIn Profile get seen by the recruiters and hiring managers at your DREAM opportunities.

FREE BONUS 4: THE DEAL SEALERS

After that, with our Fourth FREE Bonus, which is Missing Link #4, *The Deal Sealers*—I'm going to give you the Email and Messaging Campaigns you can use to build a list of High-Value References AND give you my framework on how to Successfully Navigate Multiple Offers at the SAME Time—which WILL happen for many of you going through this system.

FREE BONUS 5: THE OFFICIAL JOB SEEKERS UNIVERSITY MOCK INTERVIEW

You'll get the *Official Job Seekers University Mock Interview*—a Simulated, Real-Life Interview Environment that has Instantly Eliminated Anxiety for Hundreds of our Job Seekers and has given them the extra edge they need to go into their interview rounds with complete control and CONFIDENCE.

FREE BONUS 6: THE PRIVATE CAREER COMMANDERS GROUPS

You'll get access to our private *Career Commanders* Facebook and LinkedIn Groups (the Inner Circle)—where you can network with all current and former alumni of our program, get questions answered any time by us and by other Career Commanders who want to help you, and you can join our regular, FREE Facebook Live training on topics you choose.

Additionally, you'll also get access to our **Private "Got-It" Recruiting Service** reserved ONLY for our community of Career Commanders - where we actively search for placement FOR you as part of the Program.

WOULD THE 20 DAY JOB SEARCH PROGRAM BE WORTH IT?

Think about the value you'd gain by shortening your job search process by even ONE month. You'd gain back an entire month's salary. You'd skip the stress and uncertainty. And, by going through this system and uncovering your true Unfair Advantage, you'd increase your career earning potential ASTRONOMICALLY.

So, it would make sense for me to charge around $5,000 for my system, especially since I'm saving you an average of 4 MONTHS in your search process, right? Those 4 extra months can equate to almost **$20,000 of missed salary** for the average person!

But don't worry. I'm NOT going to charge that.

Let me ask you: If all this program did was unlock interviews for those once-out-of-reach positions, would it be worth $5,000? Or if all it did was simply erase that constant weight of job search stress, letting you sleep peacefully again, would it be worth $5,000?

Think about it. I'm sure you can agree it would be worth at least $5,000, right?

And you can see why it's a great deal at $5,000. BUT I decided to get a little crazy and give all of this away for just **$2,997** to the general public. But, as of the time of writing this book, I'm going to offer you an even better deal.

For a very limited time, you can become a Career Commander and get started now for just one payment of **$997**.

Just go to TheJobSeekersUniversity.com, select **The 20 Day Job Search Program**, enter the coupon code "COMMANDER" at checkout, and the price will drop from $4,997 down to just $997.

And of course, you get all the bonuses as well.

EVERYTHING YOU'LL GET WITH THE 20 DAY JOB SEARCH PROGRAM

In the **20 Day Job Search Program**, you'll get full, lifetime access to ALL the following.

The following 8 TRAINING MODULES:

1. Job Seeker DNA.

2. Resume Mastery.

3. LinkedIn N'sider.

4. Search Tactician.

5. ATS Hacker.

6. Networking Magic.

7. InterviewIQ.

8. The Finish Line.

The following 6 FREE BONUSES:

1. The Master Negotiator Course.

2. Our Cover Letter Blueprint Training.

3. The Bonus Cheat Codes.

4. The Deal Sealers.

5. The Official Job Seekers University Mock Interview.

6. Access to Our Exclusive Career Commanders Facebook and LinkedIn Groups AND Our Private "Got-It" Recruiting Service.

More than half of the people who have completed the 20 Day Job Search Program have multiple interviews lined up just 2 WEEKS after starting the program.

This is my VERY BEST. It's the result of YEARS of researching, organizing, building, and perfecting the ultimate system that's built for YOU. It's something that you're not going to find ANYWHERE else in the market. And I want to give it ALL to you for just one payment of $997.

So, there it is. I hope you see how passionate I am about helping you change your life and take command over your career. Make sure to visit TheJobSeekersUniversity.com and select **The 20 Day Job Search Program** to check out your special offer and several other bonuses I have for you if you order today

AUTHOR'S NOTE: ARE YOU A FIT FOR OUR DONE-FOR-YOU JOB SEARCH SERVICE?

If you're ready to take the fastest path to landing your dream job, WITHOUT the work on your end, my team of Job Search Architects and I would love to do your job search FOR you. Yes, you heard that right! Our premier, white-glove Done-for-You Job Search service is a full-scale experience designed to handle every aspect of your job search for you. The only thing you'll need to do is click the "Apply" button.

It includes expert-crafted, ATS-Certified Resumes and LinkedIn Profile builds, personalized Job Applications, a custom Networking Campaign, One-on-One Interview Preparation, and a tailored Salary Negotiation plan. Plus, you get Lifetime Access to the entire 20 Day Job Search Program, Bonuses, and exclusive Support Groups.

So if you want to find the BEST job in the SHORTEST amount of time possible, visit TheJobSeekersUniversity.com, select **The Done-for-You Job Search**, and schedule a call now. The job search is OUR job. It doesn't have to be yours!

THANK YOU!

Thank you for reading my book!

It is my sincere hope that my strategies and tips will empower you to land your dream job.

Here's my email: tommy@thejobseekersuniversity.com. Please don't hesitate to let me know what you thought of my book. Or just reach out to let me know how I can help you.

If my book has helped you land your dream job, please leave a review. Your review is very important because it'll help other job seekers learn about how this book can help them land their dream job, get paid more to do it, and take command of their career.

JOIN OUR CAREER COMMANDERS TRIBE!

To join our community of like-minded people who are taking COMMAND over our CAREERS (and gain access to some pretty awesome job opportunities), visit CareerCommanders.com and join our Career Commanders Facebook and LinkedIn groups.

CONTACT OUR EXPERTS

You deserve better than the current job search advice you're getting, and we're here to support you in going from WANTING your dream job to LANDING your dream job.

If you have any questions, email us at support@thejobseekersuniversity.com or visit TheJobSeekersUniversity.com and schedule a call.

I, along with my team of experts, will be happy to answer any questions you may have.

ACKNOWLEDGMENTS

Creating the course that this book is based on and then transforming that program into this book—wow, what a journey! I am deeply grateful to everyone who has contributed to this project and supported me along the way.

First and foremost, I want to express my heartfelt gratitude to the job seekers who have shared their stories, struggles, and triumphs with me. Your experiences have been the driving force behind my work in general and this book in particular. It is my sincere hope that the insights I share within these pages and via Job Seekers University will empower you to navigate the job market with confidence and achieve your career goals.

I extend my deepest appreciation to my mentors and advisors whose guidance and wisdom have been invaluable throughout this process. Your expertise has helped shape my programs and this book into resources that I am truly proud of.

To my family and friends, thank you for your unwavering support and encouragement. Your belief in me has been a constant source of strength, and I'm grateful for the countless hours you've spent listening to my ideas, offering pushback when I was off track, and cheering me on when I was building something worthwhile.

Thank you to the awesome professionals who have helped me create my programs and this book. Your attention to detail and commitment to excellence have been instrumental in shaping my work, all of which will go on to benefit countless other people.

I want to thank the readers of this book and the participants in my programs. It is my sincere hope that my strategies and tips will empower you to land your dream job.

Last but not least, I would like to thank my beautiful wife and kids! MaryEllen, thank you for your patience, encouragement, and belief in me. James and our future baby on-the-way, thank you for your sweet office visits and distractions full of snuggles. My love for you all is immense and unwavering.

With gratitude,

Tommy

ABOUT THE AUTHOR

"I believe that your unique experience, powered by the right system, can transform your career!"
— Tommy West

For Tommy West, the belief in this philosophy sparked the creation of the first and only job search system that's helped thousands of job seekers land their dream jobs and take command of their careers. Growing up in a family business with over 30 years of experience in job search assistance, Tommy thought his first post-college job search would be a breeze—but it wasn't. His eyes were opened to how inefficient the job search process truly was and how it's holding back millions each year from reaching their career goals.

In this, he found his purpose—to ensure no other job seeker ever had to feel the same way that he, and so many others, did again. Since then, he's worked with job seekers ranging from those just starting their careers to Fortune 500 Executives, helping them create, refine, and perfect The New Way of Job Searching. Tommy is the Founder & CEO of Job Seekers University, the world's foremost leader in job search research and solutions on a mission to free 1 million job seekers from the chains of traditional guidance.

MORE GREAT CONTENT BY TOMMY WEST

Be sure to head over to TheJobSeekersUniversity.com/our-programs/ to get your FREE Custom Master Key Report.

Our FREE 100% Custom Report ensures your application makes it past the Applicant Tracking System for the job posting of your choice. Our industry-leading Application Master Key Tool reverse-engineers the specific Applicant Tracking System at your chosen opportunity and will provide you with the EXACT keywords you need to include in your existing resume to get seen. This is your GOLDEN TICKET!

For more Free content, make sure to sign up for The 5-Day Dream Job Challenge and register for the Live Webclass hosted by Tommy West: "How to Land Your Dream Job Without Suffering Through Countless Applications or Facing Constant Rejection" at TheJobSeekersUniversity.com.